THE GUIDEBOOK TO SELF-RELEASING YOUR MUSIC

THE GUIDEBOOK TO SELF-RELEASING YOUR MUSIC

A GUIDE FOR COMPOSERS, SOUND ARTISTS AND PERFORMERS

MATTHEW WHITESIDE

Edited by
LAURA PEARSON

Important disclaimer

This publication contains materials designed to assist the reader in understanding the processes, strategies and rights involved in releasing their own music for education purposes only. While the publisher and author have made every attempt to verify that the information produced in this book is correct and up to date, the publisher and author assume no responsibility for any error, inaccuracy, or omission.

The advice, examples, and strategies contained are not suitable for every situation. The advice examples, and strategies contained are not intended to represent or guarantee you will achieve your desired results through self-releasing, and the publisher and author make no such guarantee. Neither the publisher nor author shall be liable for damages arising from following the advice and guidance contained in this book. Every business decision carries a risk of capital loss and failure.

This book is not intended for use as a source of legal or financial advice. The information contained is for guidance and education only. You should seek legal and financial advice from appropriately certified sources.

ISBN 978-1-7384581-0-3: Paperback

ISBN 978-1-7384581-1-0: Ebook

First Edition

CONTENTS

PART I

INTRODUCTION

1
—————

HOW TO USE THIS BOOK

Throughout my career I have been passionate about making music and helping others do the same. I'm a classical composer and concert producer, supporting fellow composers and musicians through lobbying, commissioning, mentoring, and providing other industry guidance. Teaching others how to develop and promote their music brings me great joy, regardless of genre.

If you are like me, you want to get your music out there in the world. You've realised that recording could give you many opportunities to showcase your music. Maybe you want to use a recording to promote a live performance or to market yourself as a composer. Perhaps you've already had some success in the music business, getting onto development schemes, a commission, artistic residencies, or teaching engagements, and you want to take your 'brand' to the next level. If you can relate to any of these goals, this book is for you.

During the pandemic, I held webinars to teach people how to release their own music; everything from producing and recording through to promotion, marketing, rights, distribution, and sales. My aim was for attendees of these webinars to know everything they needed to release their music either as a single or an album. The webinars packed an overwhelming amount of information into a 70-minute session. Participants often asked me for a reference book distilled down to the main points that would help them navigate their own self-releasing journeys. This is that book. While it is UK-centric, the skills I talk about can be applied globally. In addition, the book focuses on the most relevant topics regardless of musical genre. I have provided contact information and other resources for additional support along with a page on my website where these recourses will be collated along with other relevant things.

Head to www.matthewwhiteside.co.uk/guidebook-resources if you want to have it open while you're reading.

In this book, I share my knowledge and experience. I hope it will help you sidestep potential pitfalls, employ new strategies to promote yourself and your music, and help you find your way to a successful career in music. If you decide that self-releasing is not for you, and you opt to sign with a record label, that is totally fine as well. This book is about giving you that self-understanding and ability to enter a negotiation with a label from a place of knowledge. Knowledge that will help you secure a better deal for yourself, your career, and your business.

Releasing your own music is a lot of work! The first time I went through the process, I was overwhelmed learning about rights and registrations, budgeting and funding, the contracts I needed to sign, marketing and advertising, creating a presence on social media, and making sure everyone was in the right place at the right time with the right equipment in a quiet venue that sounded good and was affordable. It was challenging! But I was determined to sort it out and make it work. The 'prize' at the end was that I would own my music entirely. I could earn money from it and license it for synchronisation. I didn't need to share any royalties.

But releasing your own music is not for everyone. Are you sure you want to take on the work that's required for the promise of earning more income, assuming all artistic control, and a guarantee that your music will be released? Or would you rather take on less work, sacrifice artistic control, and live with the possibility that your music might never be released? Of course, you might write the next mega-hit, and you and someone else's record label would benefit greatly. These are the trade-offs you need to consider. There is no wrong answer. Each person's life situation is different. This book will help you make an informed decision about what's best for you.

As you start this process you should think about how releasing your music fits into your business goals. Do you want to earn money from it? Do you want to raise your profile to get commissions, residencies, or other funding? Or do you simply want a high-quality documentation of your work? Your specific goals will determine how much effort you will need to put into various parts of the process. If you want to develop an income stream from your released music, then you should follow the guidance throughout this book; if you want to create recordings for the purpose of seeking other commissions, you might want to invest more on PR when you release to make sure your music reaches those decision makers; or if you just want high quality documentation of your recordings you can just concentrate on the recording section. Though if you go to all that effort, why not release your music anyway?

I've used the word, 'business', a few times and will continue to do so throughout the book. I know some of you may have bristled at the word already! The music industry is a vast business set up to entertain people in exchange for money. Some parts of the business are blatantly commercial, like the pop music industry that is sustained by vast numbers of fans attending concerts and buying or streaming music. Other parts of the business can't be supported financially by audience numbers alone and rely on funding organisations to keep them going to develop the artform and the performance practice. Regardless, all music ventures require the producers and musicians to deal with the pressures of marketing to audiences, marketing to businesses (e.g., pitching a gig to a venue), making touring decisions, building release schedules, creating business development plans, and paying bills. If you can't pay the bills, you won't be able to create music. All of this sounds like a business to me. The business of art.

When I was starting out, one of the things that helped me get into the business mindset was to think of myself as Matthew Whiteside, the Composer. A completely separate entity to Matthew Whiteside, the Person. The Composer, Matthew Whiteside, didn't mind talking about his music on the internet or giving interviews about his work, and was quite outgoing. On the other hand, Matthew Whiteside, the Person, was shy and didn't want to impose his music projects onto others. In fact, he preferred to sit at home listening to and writing music, reading, watching films, and occasionally going scuba diving. This distinction helped Matthew Whiteside, the Composer, develop his music business without Matthew Whiteside, the Person, getting in the way. I realised that this is what a lot of pop artists do; they create a stage persona that becomes their business brand.

No matter what genre of music, you are a business. If you want to be a professional musician or composer, you need to think of yourself as a business. Even if you aren't completely onboard with this idea, I hope you will think otherwise by the end of this book.

So, how do you release your own music?

This book is a step-by-step guide that includes how to identify and hire the best people for your project, how to estimate costs, tips for saving money, how to apply for funding, how to plan, record, and finalise your recording for release, and how to create your unique brand and market your music to the world.

The book is roughly divided into five sections:

- Choosing the best people
- Budgeting and fundraising
- Recording, postproduction and preparing your music for release
- Public relations, marketing, branding, and synchronisation
- Perspectives on the music industry

The earlier sections focus on studio recording, working with notation-based music and recording live players. If you are a bedroom producer, this might not be relevant to your work now but will equip you for when and if you want to go this route. You'll learn the skills to work with classical players even if you aren't working with them...yet. If you are a band going into a recording studio, these chapters will help you understand all the different roles and parts of the process and how to track the development of the album.

I've included a few non–skills-based chapters, too, which cover different perspectives on the music industry, such as the ethics of streaming and conflicts of interest across record companies.

Whenever a key term is introduced, it will be written in **bold**, followed by the definition. If you come across the term again later in the book and can't remember what it means, flip to the glossary at the end of the book and you will find it there.

I've provided links to websites and other resources, including budget templates and a workbook. These are available to you on my website at <u>https://www.</u> <u>matthewwhiteside.co.uk/guidebook-resources/</u>

This book is not going to teach you how to craft a composition or write a song. It will, however, guide you through the confusing process of getting your works recorded and out into the world. The confusion isn't helped by the fact that the landscape of the music industry is constantly shifting with new services starting or businesses opening, new payment models being developed, old ones being changed, and new legislation being written.

Although I received an excellent, in-depth university and music college education on how to compose music and work with musicians, I didn't get information on the *business* of music. While many institutions are starting to offer courses and modules that teach students how to survive and thrive in the music industry, most music students are still graduating with limited understanding of making music in the 'real' world. In addition to these university graduates, a plethora of talented, self-taught producers, composers, and songwriters are creating music without any professional guidance.

This book is for *all* of you: whether you have had a formal music education or are self-taught; whether you are working in your bedroom or in a rehearsal space; whether you were given the opportunity to learn how to survive as a freelancer or are just graduating. In fact, this book is for anyone who wants to release their music or include recorded music as part of their business. I hope I can support you on your journey.

PART II

THE GUIDEBOOK TO SELF-RELEASING YOUR MUSIC

2

CHOOSING THE BEST PEOPLE

Are you planning to produce your own music, or do you want to hire a professional producer? How do you go about finding and hiring an engineer? Where do you source musicians? The people you hire will determine the quality and success of your project. Let's look at the key roles.

Producers

The **executive producer** is the project manager, coordinating all the creative and technical aspects of a recording project–an artistic hub at the centre of the spokes. The executive producer hires people, finds funding for the project, coordinates release and marketing activities, and is responsible for ensuring that the artist's vision is realised by all involved in the project.

If you are self-releasing your music, then this is you. Congratulations, you can give yourself a fancy title!

You might not want to, but this is what you are doing by organising your own release.

Executive producer skills include:

- Fundraising
- Budgeting
- Contracting
- Scheduling and Timeline Management
- Coordinating release strategies for multiple releases (mainly for a record label).

The **record producer** (or simply producer) coordinates with the executive producer regarding recording logistics and hiring decisions for the musicians and other crew. However, it is the record producer who is in the recording studio making artistic decisions and giving performance direction.

If you decide to produce your own music, you will need to manage all artistic aspects of the recording process. What skills do you need to be successful?

- Music expertise relevant to the genre you are working in. For example, high-level score reading skills for notation-based music.
- Listening skills and a keen ear for detail, such as the ability to hear differences between different mics and mic placement and how an effect or EQ setting is helping or hurting the sound and a broad understanding of post-production techniques.

- An artistic vision for the project and the ability to articulate this clearly to everyone involved (recording engineer and musicians).
- Excellent people management skills, including the ability to give constructive criticism on performance, negotiate differences in artistic opinions and resolve conflicts, and the ability to create a safe and supportive environment for everyone to create their best work.
- Excellent time management skills. The recording process is a very full-on experience, and the producer needs to manage each session to get the best performance from everyone while making sure everyone takes the breaks they need as stated within their contracts. It can be very easy for time to slip away.
- Excellent note-taking ability to keep track of different takes within the session.

After assessing your skills, you may decide you are fully capable of producing a recording yourself. But even so, you still might need someone else to do it. For example, if you plan to play your own music in a session, you will need someone to oversee the overall production and listen to your performance during the recording session. In this case, you'll need to hire a producer.

The producer needs to understand your musical genre and have the specific skills that you require. For example, if you are a classical composer or musician, you'll want a producer who is highly competent in reading scores. If you are the composer/songwriter of a band that uses electronics, you'll want someone who understands post-production processing and song structures. Or maybe you want someone who works in a completely different genre to push you in a new way of thinking and working.

Ask people you know for recommendations. Look for the producer's name in liner notes of recordings that you like. Sometimes the right producer comes from unlikely places. I knew an electroacoustic composer who produced a rock band's album because they shared the same artistic vision as the band. Find your kindred spirit. Find someone who will challenge you. Find whoever is best for the project.

Once you've identified someone, discuss what you expect them to do and ask for a cost quote. If you are producing, set a fair and reasonable fee for yourself. Use a day rate set by a relevant Union. This is most important if you are applying for external funding (e.g., the Arts Council) as they want to ensure everyone involved is paid fairly. If you don't pay everyone fairly (including yourself) this will reduce the likelihood of a successful funding application. If the producer is well-known or has significantly influenced your recording, you may opt to pay them a cut of the composition royalties. Did the producer change any of the music you wrote, such as making suggestions on melody, arrangement, phrase length or structure (like a co-writer)? This could warrant giving them points, or a percentage, of the composition royalty.

However, if the producer acted solely as a conduit for your artistic vision and a second pair of ears, a flat fee would be more appropriate. Regardless, make sure you have a written agreement with the producer before the project starts, so everyone understands expectations and responsibilities.

Engineers

A **recording engineer** is responsible for operating the audio equipment in a recording session to achieve the desired sound as stipulated by the producer.

If you're recording in a studio, check to see if the engineer is included in the cost. If not, you will have to hire your own. As with the producer, ask people you know if they have any recommendations, or look at recording credits for names. Avoid setting up commitments with people unless you've had a chance to hear their work. Your friend at the pub *might* be an amazing engineer, but it's likely they are not. Unless you know people professionally and have heard their work, steer clear of these common pitfalls. The exception to this is the inhouse engineer if the studio comes with one. They are likely very experienced, and you can be pretty sure they will do an excellent job for you (though I would still suggest asking for examples of their previous work).

Once you've hired an engineer, check that they have equipment you can use. If not, you will need to hire it separately. You could give them a budget to hire it for you as part of their fee, or you could hire it directly yourself. Recording studios will almost always come with everything you need to record.

The **mixing engineer** is responsible for mixing the recorded work. The **mastering engineer** is responsible for mastering the final recording for release. Both might work at home in their respective studios or go somewhere else to mix and master.

The recording, mixing and mastering engineer might be the same person, or you might choose to hire different people for each part. There are people that specialise in each of these areas. Later in the book I will explain why you might want to do this yourself if you have the relevant skills.

Musicians

Musicians will include any instrumentalists or vocalists you hire to perform your work. If you don't have specific musicians in mind, you are going to have to find them yourself. A producer could help source people. You could also contact individual players or an ensemble that you like and whose aesthetic matches yours. Resources like www.encoremusicians.com are an excellent way to find musicians. Ask for recommendations on social media or use a fixer.

A **fixer** is a person who books musicians for recording sessions. Fixers can be anything from musicians who book people from their personal contacts to professional fixers whose job it is to book musicians from numerous sources. You can find fixers on LinkedIn or ask a local orchestra if they can create an ensemble for you from their players. You could also search musician-sunion.org.uk for the Musicians' Union Approved Contractor list to find fixers that have agreed to work within the MU's terms and policies. If you work with one of these fixers, you know they will be quoting fair rates and musicians will be happy to be booked by them. Personal connections and introductions are always the best way to find talented people.

If you have written your music for specific musicians, schedule a recording the day after a performance of the piece so everyone is fully rehearsed. If you are working with a larger ensemble (e.g., 6+ musicians), hiring a conductor could make sessions run more efficiently and therefore cut costs by helping with timing, ensemble issues and entries. Show the musicians or conductor your music and talk to them about the complexity so you have an idea of how many sessions you need to book. This will influence the budget. To find a conductor you either need to ask musicians you know for recommendations or use Google. Most conductors have their own website and should be easy to find. But like with the other people you are hiring for the project, make sure you listen to work they have conducted before you hire them or get personal recommendations.

PR specialist

A PR specialist (sometimes called a 'plugger') is someone who will help you frame your story and share it with the world. It is important to choose the right person to work with as each PR specialist has their own focus and their own book of contacts. You can choose this person further along in the process. Chapter 12 is devoted to PR, and I will delve into this topic then.

You

You need to think of yourself as someone with a role—in fact, numerous roles—within the process. Given your schedule, budget, skill set, experience, etc., are you the best person for a particular role or roles? As someone self-releasing you are already the executive producer and record label. Likely also the composer, performer, or producer. You have many hats you could be wearing. But the two key hats that you will need to think about through this process are:

You as the composer/songwriter, the person who wrote the music and wants to get it out into the world.

You as the record label. People often think a record label needs to be a company. It doesn't. You are acting as a record label for yourself.

I will talk more about what these mean as they relate to rights and registrations, but start thinking of yourself as having multiple roles as you read through the rest of the book.

3

BUDGETING

This chapter will help you plan a realistic budget *before* you start spending and offer some ideas on how to offset your costs.

Estimating costs

Please see the sample budget spreadsheet below. The blank spreadsheet can be downloaded from my website www.matthewwhiteside.co.uk/guidebook-resources. Fill in your projected costs and earnings to create a balanced budget (we will look at how to budget for earnings in chapter 4, Funding). The numbers I have entered on the spreadsheet are rough and are not fixed to any industry standard except for the fees set out in the MU/BPI session agreement, where applicable. Most people in the music industry are freelancers and set their own fees. You will be negotiating these fees on a case-by-case basis if the freelancer wants a higher rate than the MU minimums. This applies to producers, engineers, and musicians.

Services like public relations, marketing, and advertising will have their own rates, which may or may not be negotiable. The costs are likely to change too from when this book is printed to when you are reading it because people change their rates, prices increase and every year or two the Musicians Union looks at their recommended fees. So make sure to do your research on costs and get quotes *before* starting a project.

Category	Expense	Comment	Item Cost	Item Number (e.g., days or # of sessions)	Line Total	Running Total
Production Staff	Executive Producer	Quote	£250.00	3	£750.00	£750.00
	Recording Producer	Quote	£250.00	6	£1,500.00	£2,250.00
	Recording Engineer	Quote	£250.00	2	£500.00	£2,750.00
	Mixing Engineer	Quote	£250.00	2	£500.00	£3,250.00
	Mastering Engineer	Quote	£250.00	2	£500.00	£3,750.00
Musician Fees	Musician(s)	Standard 3h session fee, 2 sessions a day, 2 days, 4 musicians. MU/BPI Agreement	£130.00	2x2x4=16	£2,080.00	£5,830.00
Venue and Equipment	Venue Hire	Quote	£500.00	2	£1,000.00	£6,830.00
	Equipment Hire	Quote	£300.00	2	£600.00	£7,430.00
Expenses	Travel	2 musicians traveling by train	£89.00	2	£178.00	£7,608.00
	Accommodation	2 musicians staying one night	£130.00	2	£260.00	£7,868.00
	Subsistence	2 musicians for 2 days	£50.00	4	£200.00	£8,068.00
PR & Marketing	PR	Quote for 4-month UK campaign	£3,500.00	1	£3,500.00	£11,568.00
	Marketing	Facebook Ads and Pre-save	£350.00	1	£350.00	£11,918.00
	Album Printing	Quote for 100 copies	£690.00	1	£690.00	£12,608.00
	Album Digital Distribution		£50.00	1	£50.00	£12,658.00
	Cover Artwork	Quote	£500.00	1	£500.00	£13,158.00
	Album design	Quote	£350.00	1	£350.00	£13,508.00
	Contingency	10% budget	£1,350.80	1	£1,350.80	£14,858.80

Sample budget spreadsheet

Musician fees and session lengths

The Musicians Union (MU), the UK Trade Union for musicians and composers, publishes fees they have negotiated with the BPI under the MU/BPI session agreement. This document is updated every few years, but the core of the agreement remains the same: you pay the musicians' fees, and you get the rights to release the music. I'll discuss this in more depth in the Rights section.

The MU/BPI session agreement can be found via a direct link on the resources page of my website.

These are the main points in the agreement as of 2023 are:

1) *THE MAXIMUM SESSION LENGTH.* As of 2023 this is a 3-hour session for £130, a 4-hour session for £194.40 and a 2-hour session for £97.20. 3-hour sessions are the standard length of recording session so you can fit two in one day.

2) *THE NUMBER of minutes of music you are allowed by the MU/BPI agreement to record in a session.* In a 2-hour session, it's 10 minutes; in a 3-hour session, it's 20 mins; in a 4-hour session, it's 30 minutes. If you have a 35-minute piece you want to record, you will need to pay for at least two recording sessions: two 3-hour sessions. You are allowed to record up to 20 minutes in the 3-hour session. This requirement holds even if you could record the 35-minute piece in one 4-hour session, you would still need

to pay for an additional 2-hour session. The table across the page summarises this information.

If your piece is difficult and needs more than one session–even if it is just 10 minutes long–you will be required to book as many sessions as you need to record the piece. If the musicians want to be paid more than the minimum, you will need to pay them what they ask or find different people. The MU/BPI rates are, like all union rates, the minimum.

Session Type	Standard Session	Long Session	Short Session
Max. Duration	3 hours	4 hours	2 hours
Max. Track(s) Duration	20 minutes	30 minutes	10 minutes
Session Fee	£130.00	£194.40	£97.20

Number of minutes you are allowed to record in a session by the MU/BPI

3) SESSION BREAKS. The musicians are due a break of 5 minutes for every hour of the session. You generally take that half-way through, though can be agreed otherwise.

4) PPL REGISTRATION. As the record label, you are obligated to register all pertinent details of the recording with PPL. I've elaborated on this in the registrations section in chapter 8.

5) INSTRUMENT HIRE and transportation (porterage). For example, if you need a marimba or a specific type of

piano, you will likely need to hire it and pay for the transportation yourself. (A recording studio doesn't usually have an in-house marimba!). The MU/BPI session agreement also stipulates porterage on some larger instruments like double bass. This is on top of any train or milage costs. Something I've only found out recently is that technically you can't take a cello on a train. The terms of National Rail carriage disallow 'large musical instruments' such as cellos or guitars.

CHECKLIST:

- How much music do you need to record?
- How difficult is the music?
- How many sessions do you need?
- Are there any instrument hire/transportation costs?
- Have you read the MU/BPI session agreement?

Travel and Accommodation

You will need to reimburse musicians for their travel expenses and travel time, including train tickets, hotel, airfare, taxis, buses, and petrol. Use HMRC's mileage expense allowance if the musicians are driving. You will also need to pay subsistence rates if working away from home to cover costs of breakfast, lunch, and dinner. The Musicians' Union has a subsistence rate in their concert fees (this changes every year) but not one in the session agreement. You are required to pay the musicians' porterage fees to transport big instruments, as mentioned earlier. These are set out in Schedule B of the MU/BPI session agreement.

Travel expenses could influence your choice of venue. For one project, I realised it was cheaper for me to travel and work in a studio closer to the ensemble than for them to travel to me. It was also much easier logistically.

Editing, mixing, and mastering

Editing, mixing, and mastering are three parts in the process from the end of the recording session to finished product. Broadly speaking, you should estimate 1 day of editing, 1 day of mixing, and 1 day of mastering for each day of recording. This can change depending on the recording session, how good your notes were, what kind of recording you are after, what genre you are working in, how much postproduction work is needed, etc. There aren't any industry standard rates for engineers like there are for performers so you will have to ask the people you want to work with to get quotes.

Contingency

Establishing a contingency is good practice for any budget. Set aside 5-10% of your budget to address any unexpected costs; for example, an increase in the cost of transportation, printing additional parts, finding a studio at the last minute because the one you booked is flooded, paying airfare for a player because your specialist oud player is sick. A contingency simply covers costs you couldn't anticipate. It can also cover lower than expected income.

VAT

Don't forget VAT when budgeting. This is usually only relevant for venue hire, PR companies and disc printing but can add 20% on top of a fee. Make sure to double check whether any quotes you get are 'Plus VAT' (meaning quote + 20%) or 'Including VAT' (meaning VAT is already included in the quote). I have been stung on this in the past and used my contingency to cover it. If you are VAT registered, you can claim VAT back, but you are likely not registered for VAT as the annual income requirements are quite high. Look on the HMRC website or talk to your accountant to understand VAT registration properly.

4

FUNDING AND EARNED INCOME

Some people are willing to make a hefty personal investment and incur a sizeable debt to get their music known. But for most of us composers and musicians, taking on this level of debt is a very risky business. The good news is that you don't need to pay for it all yourself. There are organisations that will pay, or at the very least, support you to record and release your own work if it fits with what they are interested in supporting. These organisations come under two broad categories: public funding and private funding. You will also need to calculate earned income: how your recording will earn you money to offset the recording costs.

Public funding

Public funding comes from a combination of the government and the National Lottery and is distributed by arts councils–arm's length organisations that were set up to support the arts and to reduce the risk of any political influence swaying individual project decisions. Arts councils allocate funding based on overarching priorities agreed within the legislation.

The Arts Council of Great Britain was set up in 1946 to invest in the country after World War 2. In 1994, the Arts Council was devolved into arts councils in each UK country. As of 2023, there are four arts councils in the UK: Arts Councils of England, Wales and Northern Ireland, and Creative Scotland, which was rebranded from the Scottish Arts Council in 2010.

While these arts councils have slightly different ways of working and different budgets, each of them has a core function to support the development of arts and culture through investing in the development and work of individuals and organisations. As a musician or a composer, you can apply to these organisations to support your creative work–and you should!

Creative Scotland alone awards around £1million every month across all artistic endeavours. This includes funding the recording and development of albums in all genres: bands, singer-songwriters, and rappers, as well as string quartets and orchestras...and so much more! Some funded albums have been nominated for the Mercury Prize or a Grammy. In recent years, a band that received funding to record their first album is now playing at this years' Download Festival (a yearly summer metal festival in Donnington). I have dealt mostly with Creative Scotland, but the same opportunities exist with the other arts councils.

Private funding

Private funders are harder to find but some ways easier to apply to than the arts councils, some are much harder. Some private funders will have a yearly budget of £10,000, some £10 million. Some of the bigger funders that exist for individuals would be the PRS Foundation (you can apply for up to £5,000 as an individual) or Help Musicians (up to £3,000). They both fund recordings in all genres. Other smaller funders would be Vaughn Williams Foundation (only classical) or Hope Scott Trust (focus on Scotland). Some of these funds have an application form, others require a letter. *The Directory of Grant Making Trusts and Funds* is a must-have resource when applying for funding. It doesn't need to be the most recent edition; pick up a second-hand copy from Amazon or go to your local library.

Applying for funding

You don't have to employ a professional grant-writer to secure funding, as they aren't cheap, and they require payment whether the funding is granted or not. However, fundraising is a skill that you need to learn. It will improve with practice. Although I've been working in the arts for over 10 years and have raised almost £1,000,000, my hit rate with successful applications is still around 1 in 3 or 1 in 4. So don't be disheartened by receiving a rejection. A post floats onto my social media timeline every so often that says you should aim for 100 rejections a year. This seems like a lot, but the idea behind it is to steel yourself against rejection and just get used to it as a normal part of the process. And I think it is a really good way to reframe the rejection that comes hand in hand with a career within music.

A rejection can come in any order of magnitude: you could ask for a gig or express an interest in being involved in a project and be told 'no thanks' or you could be declined for funding after spending hours writing an application for a new body of work that would set you up financially for the next 18 months. If you aren't already, get used to being told 'no'. It's just part of the process.

Funding is never guaranteed until you have signed the contract. Don't ever take positive noises from a funder as a given that you will get the money. I have made that mistake; thankfully, I hadn't yet started investing in the project. I know some people who have invested money that wasn't yet theirs, booking musicians and studios, resulting in significant financial loss and emotional fallout for everyone involved when the funding fell through.

Having said that, remember that these organisations really do want to fund your music! They want to invest in the arts–that's why they exist. I've sat on funding panels where everyone wants to fund everything but there just isn't enough money to go around and it is painful to have to make those decisions. Funding panels deciding between two different projects can be hard, so your application needs to stand out from the rest. And remember, one decline doesn't mean that a project isn't worth funding. I have just completed fundraising for a £130,000 project where I wrote 44 applications and was successful with 11. Remember to get used to being told 'no', but don't give up!

Funding tips

APPLY TO THE RIGHT SOURCE FOR FUNDING. Use common sense: If you live in Devon– apply to Arts Council of England, don't apply to Creative Scotland! If you are a rock band, go to Help Musicians or PRS Foundation– don't apply to the Vaughn Williams Foundation.

THINK CREATIVELY *on how funding sources could support your work.* When my album, *Entangled*, was being made, I was looking for funding to cover recording costs. At the time, Help Musicians didn't fund these costs (they do now), but they did offer a development fund that supported rehearsal, travel, and workshops.

I applied and received funding for travel costs and for holding two extensive workshops with the ensemble in Manchester. When it was finally time to go into the recording studio, the ensemble was well-rehearsed, significantly reducing the time required and therefore, overall cost of the recording. In a roundabout way, the fund did end up covering a good deal of the recording costs. If I hadn't been thinking out-of-the-box for how I could use this fund for my project, I would have missed the opportunity entirely.

. . .

PROJECT CONFIDENCE. Using phrases like 'I think', 'I hope' or 'if you support me' in your application are weak and project self-doubt. Instead, use phrases like 'I believe', 'I will' or 'once funded' that project self-confidence.

USE CLEAR AND CONCISE WORDING. Avoid fluff words, and unnecessary phrases and jargon. Use bullet points where possible. These guidelines will make your application easier to read and understand. Applications frequently have a word or character limit. Using concise language will help you get *more* information into your application, not less.

SUBMIT A BALANCED BUDGET. Income minus expenditure must equal £0. This includes any fee you are paying yourself for performing, recording, project managing, composing, etc. Income includes all sources of income for the project such as funding, earned income from sales or performance engagement fees if you are touring.

COMPENSATE PEOPLE, including yourself, fairly and realistically. Underbudgeting is one of the most common reasons applications are rejected. Your project might be well planned, with interesting music and respected performers, but if you cut corners on paying musicians and other key roles, you reduce your chances of being funded. It might feel odd to ask for money to pay yourself when you feel you are benefiting from the project, but you should value all your work and valuing it means paying yourself. Don't try and balance your budget by saying you will pay yourself a fee and then completely offsetting that fee with your own cash contribution. Funding panels see right through that. It is worse than just forgetting to pay yourself, you are intentionally not paying yourself, and that is not realistic or sustainable.

IN-KIND SUPPORT IS support that would have a cost attached to it, but you are getting it for free or at a reduced cost. Perhaps you have your own sound equipment you can use to record or for the tour rather than having to hire it. Or you are using a venue that is giving you the room for free or a discounted rate. In both cases you should account for the real cost (if you weren't getting it for free or a discount) in the expenditure side of the budget and then offset that cost with in-kind income. If you don't know the real cost, then look at hire companies hire sheets to give you an idea and use this figure.

USE *the application to refine your project.* Most people I speak to think of funding as this thing that you apply for once a project is fully formed, but to me, the act of writing the funding application and answering the questions helps me to understand the project better and why I am doing it. Use the application as a chance to learn about yourself, your music and what you need. Don't think of it as a bolt-on, think of it as an opportunity to reflect on the value and the focus of the project.

Check out www.resourcecentre.org.uk/information/ writing-a-funding-application/ for more detailed information on applying for funding. The Musicians' Union and Ivors Academy both offer a service to members where you can get feedback on a completed funding application before you submit it—a chance to get professional feedback before submitting the application. I am one of the Ivors advisors so if you use that service, it might be me giving you feedback!

Crowdfunding

Crowdfunding is a way to raise money for a project by soliciting a large number of people for relatively small contributions, and often promises some sort of return on investment, service or product if the project is successful. For example, I funded this book through a crowdfunding campaign and offered additional mentoring, CDs, and the published book in return. This gave me an opportunity to engage with my followers, leveraging their interest in my work and raising my profile. This is a theme throughout the book: if you ask for something from your followers or potential followers, always provide something of value in return. You need to believe that what you are selling provides more value than what you are selling it for. This approach will create loyalty and repeat business.

Keep in mind that for crowdfunding to have an impact you need to be able to reach outside of your circle or receive some additional benefit by using the platform. Otherwise, you will only be reaching people who would have supported you anyway and be giving a percentage of that support to the crowdfunding platform. You could run a crowdfunding campaign through your own website, but it would require quite a bit of work to set it up.

The crowdfunding campaign I set up for this book was particularly effective because *Creative Scotland*, the arts council in Scotland, matched any money raised: every pound pledged by someone became two pounds through the match. This meant that by crowdfunding for this book I was able to employ an editor (hello Laura!) to help me get this book into the shape you are reading today. While the crowdfunding was still reaching people who already knew about my work, there was an added benefit to running it.

Earned Income

Before you apply for any funding, you will need to estimate your earned income. **Earned income** is any income you earn from sales and streams, radio play, and synchronisation licences. If you are applying for funding, then your application should focus on expected earnings from sales and streams for one year after you release your work. Don't account for radio play or sync licences in your budget as it is highly unlikely you would get these paid in your first year. Royalties from radio play can take over a year to be paid out.

To estimate your income, you need to know the price of a sale and how much you might earn from a stream.

STREAMING

The figures in the table below are based on an average of my experience over all streaming platforms over a period of 6 months. You can use the table on the next page to help calculate estimated income.

Entity	Average Per Stream
Distributor	£0.004438
PRS	£0.00046683
MCPS	£0.0007
Total	£0.0056

Estimating earned income from streaming

This is not a fixed amount, but an average that is amalgamated through different strands and platforms through a pro-rata system. No service pays the same amount per stream every month. The current system of pro-rata payments is something I discuss more in chapter 16: The ethics of streaming.

SALE

For a digital sale through iTunes you will earn around £5. And from Bandcamp (based on a £10 sale price) you will earn £9 from a physical sale, and £8.50 from a digital sale.

£10 is a standard amount to sell CDs at concerts, you get to keep it all.

. . .

IF, in a year from release, you get 50,000 streams and sell 20 albums at concerts you will bring in about £480 from the release. That would be the estimated income on your funding application. Think of what is realistic for you based on your own experience and following.

If you are applying for a project that includes an album launch tour, you would put any ticket income or engagement fees down as income in your funding application along with any expenditure related to the concert as well. Expenditure would also include your performance and/or tour producer/organiser fee and any other relevant expenses.

My second album, totalling 40 minutes and featuring three string quartets, cost approximately £10,000 in 2019 to record, release, and market. I produced, edited, mixed, and mastered everything myself, but it was still a costly process.

CHECKLIST:

- Read the guidelines for each funding entity and only apply for what they fund
- Use the application form
- Use language that is concise and projects confidence
- Submit realistic and balanced budget

5

CHOOSING THE BEST PLACE TO RECORD

What kind of sound are you aiming for, and will the venue support it? Do you want to capture the excitement of a live performance with an audience? Are you looking for a concert hall with lots of natural room reverberation? You could always record in a traditional recording studio with very little room reverberation, giving you lots of options for post-production manipulation. What do you need to consider in each setting? You just go for the best sounding room! Right?

The best solution isn't always so straightforward.

A church would seem like a logical place for a reverberant choir sound, while a recording studio would logically seem best for a band or chamber ensemble. On my first album, I used a church with a grand piano. I went to check it out after the Sunday morning service. There wasn't any background noise that I could hear–so I booked it. A month later, I went back to record. I discovered that on weekends the background noise is non-existent but on weekdays all you can hear is nonstop traffic. If you are using a site-based venue (e.g., church) rather than a recording studio, always visit it at roughly the time you are planning to record. Traffic noise changes throughout the day and the week. Also, be aware for nearby fire stations…

If you wanted a recording in which the listeners feel as though they are sitting in a concert hall with lovely reverberant music coming from somewhere in front of them, you could achieve this in two ways: recording in a studio with reverb added in post-production, or by recording in a venue like a concert hall and having mics placed are various distances. So which venue do you choose?

If your music uses electronics of some kind, whether they are in post-production or during the performance itself, then you need to have as clean a recording as possible for processing. While de-noising software can work magic, you don't want to pick up an extraneous noise in the first place and then have to spend time and money to remove it or leave it embed into the recording.

In this chapter, I will go over the pros and cons of recording studios, location recording venues, and live recordings. I'll be describing recordings as being dry, wet, and clean. When a sound is **dry**, it refers to the 'raw' (unaltered) sound of a sound source. **Wet** is the sound after the recording is manipulated in some way. This is also true for reverberation – a dry room has little reverberation, so a sound is played and decays quickly (think a carpeted living room) while a wet room has a lot of reverberation, so a sound lingers (think a church). You will also see plugins in digital audio workstations (DAWs) with 'Wet/Dry' faders, same thing. A **clean** mix refers to a mix without distortion in which instruments or voices can be clearly heard without any unwanted noise.

Recording studio

A **recording studio** is a commercial space specifically designed for capturing, mixing, and mastering sound. In this book, 'sound' refers to instrumental, electronic, and vocal musical performances. A recording studio is the best choice for creating a dry and clean recording that can be manipulated in post-production. The hire fee will usually include all the equipment you need to record, though you might be charged extra for use of drums, amps or piano. As mentioned earlier, sometimes studios will provide the use of the in-house engineer as part of the hire fee.

Studio recordings can be manipulated in post-production to sound like they were recorded in any venue in the world (if you are intrigued look into impulse response reverb units, they are beautiful). But during the recording session itself, the dry sound can feel lifeless. It's like the difference between singing in the living room and singing in the shower. You might feel self-conscious in the living room but uninhibited in a shower that reverberates with your dulcet tones.

If you are working with performers who have never worked in a studio, explain to them what to expect, and encourage them during the recording session. Musicians accustomed to playing in concert halls often feel constrained or disoriented in this odd, lifeless acoustic. It might take some time for them to adjust. To get around this, engineers usually have a default reverb plugin they put into the mix for listening back to during the session.

Finally, what is the size of your ensemble? Few

recording studios can house an entire orchestra or choir, but most should be able to fit a string quartet.

Location recording venue

A **location recording venue** is any place you want to record that is not in a purpose-built recording studio and is not in front of a live audience. This would include churches, concert halls, theatres, event spaces, or even someone's home if you can plug a mic into a laptop.

Some concert halls will have built-in recording studios. Churches almost never do. If the venue has no facilities or limited facilities, you will need to bring in your own equipment and increase your budget to allow for the extra time to get in, set up, take down, and for hiring and transporting equipment. Ideally, you would have a space within the building as your control room separate from the musicians to prevent sound bleeding from the instruments into your headphones. This helps you hear exactly what the mics are picking up.

In a non-studio environment, the reverb of the venue is permanently 'baked' into the recording because even though you might be using a directional mic, some room sound will still be picked up from whatever surfaces it is pointed at. This would work well for an acoustic recording in a church or concert hall where reverb occurs naturally; however, the sound can't be altered as easily in post-production.

Weather can ruin a recording, even in a building that is well-insulated. I've had to contend with wind and rain battering windows and metal shutters throughout a session. Good mic placement and noise reduction strategies saved the recording, but it wouldn't have been a problem if I had chosen to record in a studio or walked outside and shook the shutters before confirming the booking to see if they might be prone to rattling in the usually lovely Glasgow weather. I won't make that mistake again!

This is not to say recording in a venue is something you should never do. Sometimes you have no choice but to use a venue because of the size of the ensemble you are recording. Or you might just like the sound of the room and want to use that in the recording. Or you feel like the musicians will give a better performance in a venue rather than in a dry recording studio. Or it might just be right for your budget.

Live recording

A **live recording** captures a live performance in front of an audience. Sound is recorded either through a feed from the mixing desk or through microphones placed strategically around the stage and venue. Live recording come with risks and challenges in managing ambient noise and performance accuracy–you can't do another take. This might be the very 'liveness' that you are aiming for...or not. I once had an ambulance going by during the quietest part of a piece I really wanted on a live album. We were able to remove the siren Doppler shifting in post-production, but it wasn't easy.

Editing live recordings is also challenging. Even if you were to record every concert in a tour, each venue would create a different sound because of differences in the shape across venues, audience size, surfaces around the venue, or changes in mic placement. This makes it very difficult to edit for consistency across performances. Not impossible, but not something you should count on being able to do.

A live recording may appeal to you because the cost is considerably cheaper than a studio and you might want the sound of an audience in the recording. But you need to understand the limitations. There is no point recording something live and realising the day after the performance you should have just spent some extra money for a studio.

Note that if you choose a live recording, you will need to budget for and pay the players a recording fee in addition to the performance fee. This is also outlined in the MU/BPI session agreement.

Choosing where to record is as much an artistic decision as a practical one. Think through the options carefully to avoid potential delays in schedule and an increase in costs. The right venue is the one that will give you the best possible recording quality within your resources. There is no wrong answer, it is your music. Do what is right for your music.

CHECKLIST:

- What is your desired recording sound?
- What is the size of the ensemble?
- Will you be using live electronics?
- What will be the challenges in the venue you've chosen?
- What background noise might you encounter?

6

PREPARING FOR THE RECORDING SESSION

O nce you've sorted the producer, venue, engineer, and musicians, you need to work out the logistics for the first recording session. The more planning and preparation you do, the smoother and more efficiently everything will run. And the more efficient the session, the less it will cost. In this chapter I'm assuming you are self-producing, but remember that you can work with someone else to produce or to assist you in any or all of these tasks.

BEFORE THE SESSION

Here's a list of tasks will need to be completed before your first session:

CONFIRM *the schedule and book the venue.* Your first action will be to confirm the schedule with all those involved, booking travel and accommodation, and making sure everyone has the parts they will be playing from (printed or digital). Contact the venue and ask what time you can get in to prepare for the session. If you need to set up equipment, ask if you can access the venue the day before. Make sure you have the phone numbers of everyone, and they have yours. You need the phone numbers in case there are any last-minute problems (delayed train, traffic jam, the studio spontaneously combusts).

COMMUNICATE EXPECTATIONS TO MUSICIANS. Make sure you or your producer have had a conversation with everyone, so they know what kind of recording you are going for: A close mic'd pop sound? A traditional classical recording? Send a link to the musicians of recordings that have the sound you're trying to approximate. This will get people into the right mindset and clarify expectations.

COMMUNICATE EXPECTATIONS TO THE ENGINEER. Talk to the engineer about anything unconventional that you're trying to achieve. Perhaps you want to add live electronics in post-production (which might change mic placement or require additional mics) or use different playing positions to achieve a varied sound by using the instrument in a different way. For example, in George Crumb's *Black Angels*, the quartet plays like a viol consort (with their instruments upside down!) and therefore needs different mic placement. What this means is that the instruments are all held more like cellos (even the violin and viola) so the sound is coming from a very different position from a normal playing position. It is your recording and music; you are responsible for preparing your engineer as best you can.

TROUBLESHOOT AND MARK up the score. Go through the scores of the music to troubleshoot any problems, working out editing points ahead of time. You might want to do this with your engineer. I've included an example below of how I mark-up a score. You can do this on either hard copy or on an iPad. You may know your music inside and out, but in the stressful environment of a recording session, having a note to yourself can be very useful. In fact, this could be your biggest timesaver. And in recording sessions, time is money.

Figure 6.1 shows the page from my marked-up score from the recording session of my *Quartet No. 4, (Entangled),* commissioned by the Institute of Physics for the 2018 Northern Ireland Science Festival. I wanted to record the whole of the first page in one take. In advance of the session, I marked up some easy edit points within the music so that I would know, if there were an issue in bar 26, the best pick-up point would be bar 18. These mark-ups may seem painfully obvious in the calm environment of home, but in the stressful environment of a recording session with multiple people waiting on your decision, your brain just might not work. Any mark-ups that can save even a few seconds are valuable.

Figure 6.1 Marked-up score from my, Quartet No. 4 (Entangled)

Print signature pages from MU/BPI session agreement. Print signature pages from the Musicians' Union/British Phonographic Industry session agreement for each musician to sign at the end of the recording session. Then print a few more in case someone makes a mistake, water gets spilt on it, or the dog eats it. **Make sure all the musicians sign the MU/BPI form before they leave the session.**

Day of the session

The day of the recording session is the day you've been planning for a long time. You might be feeling stressed. Don't worry. This is normal because you care deeply about what you are doing. Everyone has agreed to turn up and do the best job they can in service to the recording. Your job is to support them by making each person feel as comfortable and as welcome as possible.

Paying attention to the little things in a session. Food and drink can have a big impact on how welcomed everyone feels. On the way to the recording venue, pick up some biscuits, fruit, coffee, tea, and milk. Worst case, you won't need them because the venue already has supplied them, or people have brought their own. It is a simple gesture, but it gets everything off on the right foot. Plus, everyone loves a biscuit!

Be early. Make sure you get the train before the one that would get you there on time. This is partially to make sure you aren't late and partially to get ahead of any problems. This is even more so the case when you are having to move equipment into a non-studio venue (like a church/concert hall) and get it set up. The ideal would be to set up the day or evening before, but this isn't always possible. This is your recording session, take responsibility for it.

When you get there, if it is a recording studio, the engineer will already be there before you and will have started to set things up based on what you told them you wanted. Chances are they will have printed out your email with the ensemble info and any of the quirks you mentioned and going about setting up the mics and plugging things in. They might have some questions for you about what way people will be sitting or what orientation to have them in the room. Likely they will have a suggestion on where to seat people based on their experience in the studio. Use this as a starting position. Offer to grab a coffee while they are plugging things in or if you know what to do, offer to help.

The musicians will begin to arrive 15-30 mins before the session start time. Welcome them. Say hello individually and greet them by name, but this depends on the size of ensemble. Show them into the live room, introduce them to the engineer (and producer if they aren't already saying hello, too) and check they are happy with the setup and with their chairs. Different instrumentalists have different preferences for chairs: brass and woodwind players are generally happy with any 'normal' chair, cello players often need a higher chair so prefer piano stools, and double bassists usually bring their own stools. Offer some tea or coffee and biscuits. The musicians will want to warm up. Let them do this in the live room so they get a feel for the space but make them aware they might have to move to allow for mic placement or cables being run around them.

We are about 5 mins away from the agreed session start time. The musicians are getting settled in the live room and probably still warming up. Likely they are practicing little bits of the piece (I love this, hearing the first fragments of my work in the studio). Give them a five-minute warning. They might ask you a few questions about their part they noticed when practicing the night before, answer them. Don't wait, it will save time.

You will probably be getting very stressed. Don't worry. This is normal. Remember that everyone is there to do the best job possible and to support each other in making that happen.

No matter how many times I've been through this process, whether it is my music or someone else's, I get stressed.

You glance down at your watch, and it is time.

You push the talk back button.

'Good morning, everyone, let's get started'.

The musicians blatantly ignore you. They continue warming up and practicing. Your stress and self-doubt start to get the better of you. You start to question 'are they are here just to get the money and run?!' It's going to be a disaster!

The engineer leans over, turns a fader, and says, 'Sorry, forgot to turn up talk back'.

And so, you try again: 'Good morning, everyone'.

'Good morning'!

They wait for your direction.

'Let's get started from bar one and carry on through to bar thirty, please'.

'Let us know when you are rolling'.

'We already are, take it away when you are ready'.

The music starts. Take one has begun.

* * *

During the session

The next 90 minutes, up to the first break, will fly by. You will be concentrating so hard, listening to the music, taking notes, and engaging with the players. You need to manage the time and make sure it isn't wasted on needless things.

TALKBACK AND MONITORING

Talkback refers to the way the producer in the recording booth communicates with those in the live room during the recording session. Producers can use one of two methods to provide talkback: 1) through an intercom system via a speaker in the live room; or 2) by providing headphones to all of the musicians. Both options have benefits and limitations as they pertain to monitoring and subsequently, to the overall quality of the recording.

Having talkback through a speaker in the room allows the players to hear themselves and each other clearly while they are performing but you won't be able to use a click track, a guide track, or other recorded performances (if multi-tracking) that could help musicians keep to tempo, queue their entrances, etc. If these kinds of tracks were played through the in-room speaker, they would be picked up by the microphones and recorded, rendering the recording useless.

On the other hand, using individual headphones

would allow musicians to hear a click or guide track but wearing headphones could change their perceptions of their own sound, causing them to adjust in a way that negatively affects the recording or feel uncomfortable with their own sound. Using headphones for monitoring allows musicians to ask for a personalised mix. For example, singers might want to have the guitar louder than drums in their headphones to make it easier for them to tune while also hearing the rhythm.

You will have to weigh the benefits and drawbacks of the different talkback/monitoring methods to suit the needs of your project.

MIC PLACEMENT AND EXTRA NOISE

Microphones do not pick-up sound in the same way your ears do. Your ears are informed by what you are looking at. Think of talking to someone in a crowded room where everyone is talking, you can generally hear the person you are talking to clearly. Your eyes are helping.

In the control room, you might hear extra sounds that you don't want, like the squeak of a chair as the player moves, a rattle in the instrument, a hum of an amp someone left on during the last session or any number of things. Find the extraneous sound and do what you can to fix it as early as possible. You don't want to be stuck with that sound embedded in your recording. De-noising is a wonderful thing, but it can take time and you want to get the best recording you can possibly get in the session.

Similarly, if you aren't happy with the sound the

microphones are picking up, then you need to change it as early as possible. This is not something that can be changed in post-production. A small move can have a big impact on the sound.

You need some experience with recording and the underlying physics to fully understand the difference mic positioning makes. Think of a microphone as a magnifying glass for sound: it will amplify the sound wherever you point it. An instrument is a resonating body. The sound of each instrument is different because of the design, the grain of the wood or the glue used or any number of other tiny things. If you point a microphone at a specific part of the instrument, it will sound different from pointing at another part.

If you have a friend that plays acoustic guitar, ask them to play something and kneel in front of them with one ear close to the instrument. Move from the bridge, down the neck, to the sound hole and back up. You will hear subtle changes in the sound based on where you're listening on the guitar. If you do this with a microphone, the effect is even more pronounced. This is what I mean about mic placement. And this changes for every single instrument. For example, in woodwinds, the whole body of the instrument resonates. Only the lowest note will sound from the bell, every other note will resonate through the whole body of the instrument.

If you aren't getting the sound that you want on during a recording, don't assume it is the fault of the musician. Always check first that the mic placement is correct. Consult with your engineer to check the mics and move them if necessary. For example, if you are recording a flute and the sound is rather thin, it could be that the mic is pointed toward the head of the instrument rather than at the body or with a violin you are getting a lot of finger noise, the mic is likely pointed at the finger board. This is the kind of knowledge that only comes from experience. However, as with everything in music, there are artistic choices to be made. You might want the sound of fingers tapping within the recording. In my *Three Pieces for Bass Clarinet and Electronics* I want key-clicks to add a percussive element to the music so when we were recording it we had a mic set up to pick up the sound of the key clicks.

If you are working with a chamber ensemble, you should invite them into the control room after the first take to make sure they are happy with their sound. They might have some useful comments or thoughts that could inform their playing or the session in general. You want to make sure everyone is onboard before diving into a multi-day recording session. A word of warning, be wary about spending too much time on mic placement. It can eat away at your recording time.

I described the microphone as a kind of magnifying glass for sound. Different types of microphones have different defined patterns for picking up sound – the pickup patterns. I've added some of these to the resources page on my website and described them a little below.

- **Omni-directional microphones** (omni's) pick up sound within a 360-degree radius from the grill.

- **Cardioid microphones** pick up sound in the front 180 degrees of the grill.
- **Hypercardioid microphones** pick up sound in the front and most of the back of the microphone.
- **Figure of Eight microphones** pick up sound equally in the front and back of the grill. The pattern it creates looks like a figure of 8.

TAKING NOTES

You need to take detailed notes during the recording session to make sure that the next stage, the edit, is as easy as possible. Your first instinct might be to scribble or type notes that are as descriptive as possible. Don't do this. I use a system of crosses and ticks beside the take number. Something like:

- T1 B1-30 √
- T2 B1-30 XX
- T3 B1-30 √√√
- T4 B31-79√√√
- T5 B79-96 X
- And so on…

Written out in full this means:

- Take one. Bar one to bar 30. It was ok.
- Take two. Bar one to bar 30. It was really bad.
- Take three. Bar one to bar 30. It was amazing.
- Take four. Bar 31 to bar 79. It was amazing.
- Take five. Bar 79 to bar 96. It wasn't good.

You can use this system for non–score-based music very easily too. In that instance it could look something like this:

- T1 rhythm intro √
- T2 rhythm intro X
- T3 rhythm intro √√√
- T4 rhythm v1 √√

Written out in full meaning:

- Take one. Drums intro section. It was ok.
- Take two. Drums intro section. It was really bad.
- Take three. Drums intro section. It was amazing.
- Take four. Verse one. It was good.

With this system, it is easy to see that takes three and four are the best ones and should be used as the basis of the first edit.

Another option I use is shown in Figure 6.2, overleaf.

FIGURE 6.2 IS the first page of Timothy Cooper's, 'The Narrow Way', which I co-produced with Timothy for TNW Music. The 'T' lines represent the durations of different takes; the numbers represent the take number as saved in the ProTools session; and the circled and high-lighted numbers are the take number chosen for the first edit. The ticks above the numbers mean 'good take', the tildes above the numbers mean 'iffy take', and a cross-through means 'bad take'. It might look chaotic, but like any note taking system, if it works for the note taker then it is fine. It is easier to read in the colour version which you can see on my website <u>www.matthewwhiteside.co.uk/guidebook-resources</u>.

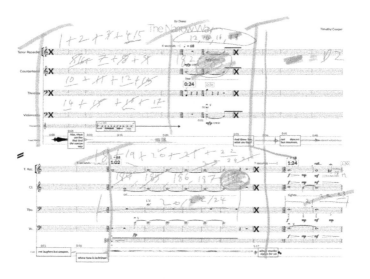

Figure 6.2 Marked-up score from Timothy Cooper's, The Narrow Way. Reproduced with permission.

THESE ARE JUST TWO EXAMPLES. Find a system that works for you that is fast and contains all the information you need to build an edit. It is important to keep notes–even of bad takes–because there might be something useful in that take in the edit stage.

TRACKING RECORDING DEVELOPMENT

When working with score-based music, I can see from my notes that we have covered the full piece and I can then set the score to the side in a 'done' pile. But you might not be working with score-based music – you might be a band or a folk singer recording an album where you are laying down a rhythm track and then multi-tracking the other parts on top of that. This requires a different kind of note taking so it is slightly harder to track where you are in the process and how much of the piece or album you have recorded. Below is a simple example of how keep on top of where you are with the album's recording process:

Song for You					
	Drums	Bass	Guitar	Fiddle	Vox
Intro	√	√	√		
Verse One	√	√			
Chorus	√	√			
Verse Two	√				
Chorus	√				
Outro	√			√	

Tracking recording development for non–score-based music

At-a-glance you can see that you've got drum takes for the whole song that you are happy with, you are halfway through the bass line, you've got the guitar's intro and the fiddle's outro but you haven't started recording any of the voice.

Recording doesn't have to be a linear process where you start from the beginning of a track and work to the end. Sometimes it makes sense to jump between parts for various reasons including stamina (if it's a hard vocal part and someone needs a break for a little or to sing an easier part), or motivation (someone is getting frustrated they can't get it right so need a break to regroup), etc. This kind of tracking gives you an overview of where you are and allows for that flexibility of jumping between sections.

LISTENING BACK

Do not listen back to a take during a session or you will be wasting time. The only time I listen back is if I have heard the same problem at the same point multiple times. For example, I once worked with a singer who, after three takes, consistently sounded wrong in one bar but I couldn't work out what I was hearing that was wrong during the performance. I had to listen back during the session to work out that the quality of the singer's voice changed during a sustained note without any indicated inflection written in the music. And I knew this wasn't a technical problem; for example, it was too long a note for them to hold and they were running out of breath.

The piece was a flexibly notated work where the tempo was indicated by time markings rather than beat markings and instead of a conductor, there was a massive clock on a screen. To ensure everyone stayed together, they needed to keep an eye on the clock for key moments. And this was the problem. The singer was moving his head to see the screen to make sure he was holding the note for the right duration. This movement was enough to change the way the mic was picking up the sound of his voice and making it sound 'wrong'. Once we realised what was going on we found a work-around: We had one of the other players give the singer the timing cue and he nailed it on the next take. If I hadn't listened back to that section to work out exactly what was going on we would have been going over the same segment numerous times, frustrating everyone.

The only time I would suggest listening back is during part of your breaks. If you have been taking good notes, your engineer should be able to piece together an edit within seconds while everyone else is making a coffee.

Just make sure you and the engineer save a good part of the break time for yourselves. Ear fatigue can be a real problem during recording sessions. During your first recording you'll likely think you'll be able to listen to a rough edit in the evening when you get home. Nope. The last thing you'll want to do after a recording session is listen to more music!

MOTIVATING PEOPLE

I mentioned earlier that you need to keep everyone upbeat and engaged during the session. Small gestures can go a long way, like offering coffee, tea, and biscuits over multiple sessions and long days. Let the musicians listen back to themselves after an early take to make sure they are comfortable with their sound. Keep the group motivated, comfortable, and productive or you risk undermining the group's confidence and goodwill.

Everyone wants to work in a nice environment and this will help them do their best work.

In the control room, you will hear things in a different way from the players in the live room. Your job is to give feedback to players in a supportive way to make sure their performance is as good as it can be. If you feedback information in the wrong way or at the wrong time, it can be detrimental to the entire session.

For example, if one of the players makes an obvious mistake, don't single out that player. Instead, say 'Let's do another take'. Everyone knows that the mistake was made, and nothing is gained by humiliating the player. On the other hand, if the ensemble isn't quite together in a section or an entry, mention what and where the issue is. With experience, you will learn when it's appropriate to speak and when it's best to stay silent.

When giving constructive feedback, always frame it positively. For example, 'That was great, but could we do another take? You didn't seem together in bar 104.' You are communicating to the players that they are doing a great job, there is nothing about the interpretation or their playing that is bad or wrong, but there's a specific bit you want to fix by doing another take.

Always provide a reason for wanting to record another take. The reason could be as simple as that you want another option for the edit but you need to be explicit about this with the players. This will save time, not leave it open for discussion, and keep people on side. If you ask for another take too often, it could undermine the players' confidence. It is a balancing act.

I've been in the control room with a composer, an

accomplished performer and session musician in their own right, who was asking for another take and giving no reason (even though I've been in sessions with them where they complained about producers requesting another take without explaining why!). I made this mistake often when I was starting out. I hope that by sharing my mistakes it will make it a little less likely you will, too. Though you probably will. It's all part of the learning process!

DOCUMENTATION

Take photos during the recording session, maybe some videos too. If you have the budget, engage a photographer so you don't have to remember to take them yourself (this is something I often forget to do). You will use those images when marketing your release later in the process. However, you don't need to engage a professional to do this. Selfies or short behind the scenes videos that you take yourself can often be as engaging, if not more so, than a professional photograph. Do what works for you, within your budget, but make sure you do something.

Final thoughts on recording day

Recording sessions will always go by faster than you think. Even if you have multiple sessions, over multiple days, do not let your concentration lapse. Don't be tempted to go to the pub after the first session–you'll regret it in the next day's session. Use the time as best as you can to protect your budget. Each player costs 72p a minute, minimum, in a standard session. If you have 10 players, that is £7.20 a minute. An orchestra of 80 is around £55 a minute. And these figures don't include room hire or any other fees.

Use the time wisely. Time is money.

Make sure you get everyone to sign the MU/BPI session agreement before they leave. If you don't have a signed copy of the agreement from everyone, you don't have the rights to release the music. Pay the musicians only after they have signed the agreement. The end of the session is the best time to get a signature off everyone.

Enjoy the left-over biscuits. You've now got your music recorded and ready to take onto the next stage. Congratulations!

7

POSTPRODUCTION

At this point you have everything recorded; you are pleased–if a little tired–with how the day went. You have the ProTools sessions on a hard drive and are ready to start the postproduction process. **Postproduction** is the name for the whole process of taking the raw, recorded music and preparing it for final release. Editing, mixing, and mastering are the three distinct parts of the postproduction process. You could hire the same person to do all three, or you could hire a separate mastering engineer to provide a fresh pair of ears. A word of caution: Unless you are experienced working with ProTools and understand how to shape the sound, then it is best to hire someone who is...especially if you are on a tight deadline. The recording studio or engineer you used would likely be able to provide postproduction services or suggest people if you don't have someone in mind already. It is entirely up to you and your budget.

It can be easy to combine the edit and mix stages but, especially when you are starting out, you should differentiate between them to help with your own understanding. The easiest way to think of the separation between edit and mix is to think of the edit as things you would tell a musician to do differently ('play it faster') while the mix is something you would tell the person behind the sound desk at a gig ('can you turn the vocals up').

Editing

Editing is the first stage of postproduction, and its purpose is to create one performance from all the takes from the recording session. An engineer will work with you, using your notes to create a rough edit. If you took good notes, this rough edit could be quick to piece together and be done on the day of recording. If you took bad notes or no notes at all, you are going to have to listen through each take to decide which to keep and which to cut. This is why taking notes during the recording session matters: You could have a swift first edit or you could spend 12 hours or more listening back to recordings (and taking notes after the fact). And if you can't run ProTools yourself, that will mean having to hire someone to help run the software for you for hours because you didn't take proper notes during the session. It's a costly mistake.

Once you've got a rough edit, you can listen back and check if you are happy with how it sounds. If you find sections that you want to fix, you can refer to your notes to find another take of the same section and decide which is the best. Again, good notes enable you to quickly find other options, so you don't have to trawl through every recording.

When discussing edits with your engineer, be clear on what you are hoping to achieve. Your engineer will be able to advise on how possible (or not) a suggested edit is. If you are working with an engineer who can read music, you might send them a marked-up score, such as Fig 6.2 in the previous chapter, with additional notes to support your editing comments.

If your engineer doesn't read music or you aren't working with notated music, then you will have to use timecodes. In this instance, your feedback notes might look like this:

Piece One

- 0 to 1min 20: take 2
- 1min 20 to 1min 30: take 6
- 1min 30 to 1min 35: take 2 (covering missed entry at 1min 32)
- 1min 35 to end: take 6

The first edit provides a broad brush stroke of how the performance will sound. The next step in the editing process is to focus on the detail. There might be a missed entry or an extraneous sound in the middle of a take you thought was perfect. If this happens, you will need to find another take that covers the problematic bit and suggest new edits to the editor. In this part of the process, you want to be clear and specific about the reason for the new edit because there might be technical reasons that your suggested edit won't work. If the editor understands what you're aiming for, they can work around it. What I'd suggest is saying something like this:

> "15sec to 20sec use take 1. I'm trying to fix the players not coming in together at 17sec."

You might go through four or five different stages of edits. Use a sensible naming structure for the files such as "[piece name]-edit-[date]". Avoid this common naming mistake:

- "[piece name]-mix 4"
- "[piece name]-mix 5"
- "[piece name]-final mix"
- "[piece name]-final mix 2"
- "[piece name]-final mix 3"

We've all done it. And probably will do it again...

How you communicate your intentions in this section will vary. You could be emailing or sitting beside your editor in the studio. The key thing is you have good notes from the initial recording sessions that you can refer to and that you communicate clearly.

Mixing

Mixing shapes the sound of the edited recording, making sure the performance sounds as good as it can within the context of the project. Mixing can be simple or a long, drawn-out process depending on many factors, like the genre you are working in, the acoustics of the room, the type of instruments that are being played, etc. Mixing could be as simple as pulling up the faders and finding a nice balance for the ensemble, or it could be extremely tedious; for example, adding postproduction electronics, removing background noise, or doing something unconventional with the mix.

One general rule is that the better the room and the recording, the less work will be needed in mixing. For example, a nice acoustic will likely need less artificial reverb while a noisy room will need more work to remove extraneous sounds, bad mic placement will require more EQ work, etc.

For most of the recordings I'm involved in—and especially my own work—I see the mix as another opportunity to shape the music with my artistic choices. One of the most obvious has to do with the movement of sound within the sound stage. While I'm writing this, I'm listening to a perfect example to explain what I mean...

In Dawn of MIDI's album, *Dysnomia* (it is a great album—listen to it), one of the mix techniques they use is to separate the attack of the piano from the resonance. You hear the piano note attack in the left speaker and the resonance moves from this left attack to the right before the next attack returns suddenly in the left before moving right again. This repetition creates a mesmerising experience and is a beautiful way to create movement in the mix that suits their music and amplifies the composition. It isn't overused and is a subtle effect that you feel on first listen but don't necessarily understand until you've listened to it several times. This is the kind of detail you can think about at the mix stage as well, if the music you are working on asks for it.

You'll also be adding more volume control elements in this stage such as limiting, compression and EQ as well as adding reverb and other effects to make the performance sound better–whatever 'better' means to your music, the performance, your recording, and the project.

The mix stage is also where using a reference recording can come in. If you are writing music like Dawn of MIDI's, use their album as a reference for the mix. You can play it for the engineer and discuss how you want to use the same effect. This is a clearer and more efficient means to communicate what you want rather than describing it in words.

Be warned, though, that priming the engineer with the wrong recording can increase the length of time required to the mix the project. On a *The Night With... Live* album, I sent Timothy Cooper, my frequent collaborator and who has engineered all TNW Music albums, a recording of something I was listening to and told him that I loved the detail and the closeness in the recording. He took that to mean that I wanted the whole next album to sound like that. I hadn't been clear that I knew some of the pieces on the album wouldn't work well with that kind of mix. After a few backwards-and-forwards of mixes, we realised where the problem had stemmed from. The mix he thought I wanted was fighting what the music needed. Once we realised this, the mix went a lot more smoothly.

I'm continually struggling with wanting my *The Night With...* releases to sound like the listener is sitting in the middle of the ensemble or very close to the solo player–a performance just for them. But because of the pieces we record and the fact we often do live recordings, this doesn't always work. With any recording project, you need to find the right balance between artistic expression and audio practicality to achieve the best sound. The 'right' balance is going to differ for every project and the 'best' mix might change from one day to the next. Music is subjective. Mixing is subjective. Do what you believe is right for your project. Trust your ears.

Mastering

Mastering sets the right dynamic in the edited and mixed recording and prepares it for final distribution on the specific platform or format for your release.

Each digital platform has a slightly different dynamic range. For example, Spotify requires a loudness level of -14dB LUFS with a headroom of 1dB while Apple Music requires -16dB LUFS. If your recording sits outside of these loudness levels, the platform can automatically add volume controls onto the recording. These changes are outside of your control and will change how someone experiences your music. And if what you've just read sounds like gobbledygook, then you will need a mastering engineer, even if you have done everything else yourself up to this point.

Mastering engineers will understand these technical issues. They will be aware of the most recent platform updates and will give you a master that is at the appropriate dynamic level, so the platform won't add volume controls once you've uploaded it.

Unfortunately, when self-releasing, you can release only one master across all platforms. Generally, I master to Spotify levels, but you can choose whichever you want.

Something else to bear in mind at this stage is to tell your mastering engineer what format and quality you need the tracks delivered in. CD printers expect 44.1khz, 16bit, Wavs. While digital distributors might take the same file quality as CDs, some might want 320kbps MP3s. Decide on your distributor well in advance so you can address these issues without compromising your release date.

8

UNDERSTANDING YOUR RIGHTS

You finally have a beautiful recording of your music, and you can't wait for the world to hear it! But before you can release it into the world, you will need to choose your distributor, finalise artwork for your product, register your recording, get your **International Standard Recording Code** (ISRC) and your **Universal Product Code** (UPC). The amount of administrative work can be overwhelming. Where do you start? Royalties.

Royalties

Royalties are collected whenever work is exploited. Exploited is a word that has quite a negative connotation around it but when it comes to the exploitation of intellectual property, it simply means that a work is being used. When someone performs, uses or buys your composition or recording, monies are collected from concert venues and online or digital storefronts by various Performance Rights Organisations (PROs) or your digital distributor and are paid to you. These organisations will track where your music is being played, request and receive royalties on your behalf, and manage the accounting of it (so you don't have to). Throughout this chapter I mention only UK-based PROs. If you are reading this book from outside of the UK, you can still join the UK PROs wherever in the world you are. However, you might prefer to join a local collecting society which exist in most countries of the world. There are links to these lists on my website www.matthewwhite side.co.uk/guidebook-resources.

Royalties are assigned on whether your work is copyrighted as a composition, a recording, or a performance. A **copyright** is a type of intellectual property right that gives the owner the exclusive right to sell, distribute, adapt, and perform a creative work. According to both UK and US law, the copyright belongs to the owner of the work and is assigned when it is recorded in tangible form (on paper or a voice note, a word document, a recording session file etc.). If you create a composition, you own the copyright. If you pay to create a recording, you own the copyright for that recording. If you record someone else's composition, but pay for the recording, you own copyright of the sound recording, but will have to pay royalties to the owner of the composition. If you pay for the recording of your own composition, you will receive royalties for both the composition and the recording, and you would be acting as your own record label. The performers are also paid a separate royalty whenever the sound recording is broadcast, called equitable renumeration in UK law.

Record label

A **record label** is an individual or company that funds the recording of music and promotes and sells it in various formats to make a profit. You won't need to set up a separate company if you are acting as your own record label. Income will be classed and declared as you would any other self-employed income (including offsetting the expenses to record).

When a work (recording or composition) is created in a tangible form in the US or the UK, it is copyrighted in the name of the original author. Registering your copyright with an official body is a way to prove your ownership in a more formal way. The Musicians' Union provides a service to members by keeping digital copies of composers' original music, thus proving a work existed at a certain time if copyright ownership was ever questioned. In the United States, the US Copyright Office is the government body that deals with copyright registration.

The Performing Rights Society (PRS)

The **PRS** protects copyright and collects royalties for composers and rights holders for live performances on TV, radio, and online streaming. When a composition is performed in public, PRS collects a royalty from licensed venues that is then paid to the composer. Even if your music hasn't been performed yet, you should join PRS and register every work you create. PRS charges a one-off joining fee but, this is an investment in your career: it ensures you will get paid whenever your music is performed and will protect you from losing out on any backdated royalties.

I keep a spreadsheet of every performance or broadcast I know of. When a royalty statement comes in, I match the income to those performances. If I haven't seen a royalty 18 months after the performance, I contact PRS through their online query system to chase it for me. It's a lovely surprise when money appears in my account from performances or from broadcasts I didn't know about.

I use the following spreadsheet to track my recordings and performances. I suggest you do the same.

Claimed	PRS Date Paid	Title	Date	Time	Venue	City/Show	Country
√	15/10/2020	Quartet No. 6	29-Sep-19	11.24pm	DR P2	Tigermoths	Denmark
√	15/10/2020	Quartet for Violin, Viola, Cello and Double Bass	09/10/2019		Maxim, Kuopio		Finland
		Quartet No. 4	27-Oct-19	5pm		Recent Releases	Australia
	15/07/2020	Response Two	15-Nov-19	11.22pm	DR P2	Tigermoths	Denmark
		Response Two	22-Nov-19		Resonance FM	Wavelength	UK
	15/12/2020	Quartet No. 6	22-Nov-19		Resonance FM	Wavelength	UK
		Spinning	22-Nov-19		Resonance FM	Wavelength	UK
		Quartet No. 5, III	22-Nov-19		Resonance FM	Wavelength	UK
√		Quartet No. 6	18-Jan-20				Canada
√		Quartet No. 6	10-Jan-20		RCS		UK
√		Quartet No. 4	10-Jan-20		RCS		UK
√	15/07/2020	Solo for viola d'amore and electronics	8-Oct-19		Hug and Pint		
√	15/12/2020	Solo for viola d'amore and electronics	9-Oct-19		Scottish Storytelling Centre		
√	15/12/2020	Solo for viola d'amore and electronics	10-Oct-19		Belmont FH		
√	15/07/2020	Solo for viola d'amore and electronics	21-Oct-19		Blackbox		

Spreadsheet to track recordings and performances

Go to www.prsformusic.com for full up-to-date information on joining and registering your music.

The Mechanical Copyright Protection Society (MCPS)

MCPS licenses and collects royalties on behalf of composers and rights holders for when works are **mechanically reproduced**; that is, reproducing a copyrighted work by mechanical means rather than creating the work in the first instance. When MCPS was founded in 1910, 'mechanically reproduced' meant piano rolls. Now it includes:

- physical products (CDs, DVDs, vinyl, etc)
- streamed and downloaded reproductions
- broadcast on TV, film, games, and advertising
- radio broadcasts
- other non-linear streams (BBC iPlayer, Netflix etc)

MCPS have a service agreement with PRS to manage and administer mechanical rights, but you still need to join MCPS *separately*. When you register works on the PRS website they will automatically appear on the MCPS database. It seems automatic from a member's perspective, but a huge team at PRS and MCPS deal with database management. I've been in their offices and was surprised by how many people were there.

Join MCPS if your music is released or about to be released. Royalties will be owed to you when your music is reproduced, and you want to get ahead of that to make sure you don't miss out on any payments. Like PRS, you'll need to pay a fee to join.

Visit www.prsformusic.com for full up-to-date information on joining and registering your music from a mechanical point of view.

Before we move on, I want to dive into the phrase 'when your music is reproduced' because it can be a bit confusing. Mechanical reproduction can take many forms. For example, let's say a company wants to create a physical product that features your music. This might be a CD, but could also be a toy that plays a tune, or a DVD. In this instance, a company would approach MCPS to acquire a license for the music they want to include in their product. They would pay that license fee before they create or sell any products. That license fee would then be distributed to the rightsholders. I talk about this style of licensing in more depth a little later.

Another way is through streams. The streaming companies (both music and film) report their broadcasts and pay a license fee to both MCPS and PRS. This licence fee is this distributed to the rightsholders through MCPS and PRS' distribution policies.

The bottom line is if your music is properly registered with MCPS, you will get royalties whenever your composition is used.

Phonographic Performance Limited (PPL)

PPL collects and distributes royalties on behalf of both the record label and performers whenever the audio recording of the work is used on TV, radio, or for streaming. And like PRS and MCPS, PPL has reciprocal agreements with other agencies across the world, such as Sound Exchange in the US.

The royalty payments are made to the master rights holder (the record label) and the performer(s) featured on the recording. If you are releasing your own music but not performing it, you would join PPL as a master rights owner only. If you are performing on someone else's recording, you would join as a performer. If you are a performer on recordings of your own music, you would join PPL both as a master rights holder and as a performer: two separate registration forms.

PPL says that "...a 'performance' generally includes all audible contributions to the recording (such as guitar or vocals). In addition, certain inaudible contributions (such as the contribution made by a conductor or studio producer) may also be treated as a performance, where the conductor/studio producer conducts or provides a similar musical direction to another performer's live performance as it is being recorded."[1] This means that if you were to perform live electronics on your music, you are considered a performer and should join PPL. However, your postproduction engineers are unlikely to be providing musical direction, so wouldn't be members of PPL.

Currently, PPL doesn't have a joining fee for master rights holders or performers but that could change. Go to www.ppluk.com for all up-to-date information on joining.

Music publishers

In addition to publishing sheet music, **music publishers** often license and market compositions for all media, including film, television, and advertising. They also manage rentals and distribution, monitor song usage, and distribute some royalties. Publishers tend to focus their resources on compiling and promoting song catalogues, rather than on composers and classical works. Though classical publishers still exist, they primarily deal with creating and selling printed music and hiring parts for orchestral performances. Publishers will pitch music to performers but, unless the performer is involved in the composition of the work, won't make any payments to performers.

Assuming you are a PRS member, the only rights you could legally sign over to a publisher would be sheet music rental, distribution, and sales. PRS would have an exclusive agreement with you to collect performance rights on your behalf. However, if you signed with a publisher, the publisher could still collect up to 50% of your performance royalties directly from PRS. This is the publisher's share. PRS explicitly state on their website that, '*PRS for Music* will not accept agreements that entitle the publisher to more than a 50% performance share'[2].

I am often asked by composers how to get a publisher rather than how they could benefit from a publisher. Publishers likely will be interested in you only after you've achieved a level of commercial success. They don't typically provide a good return on investment when you are just starting out. However, there are some publishers who work on behalf of self-releasing composers and songwriters, such as Sentric, who will do some of the same kind of work for you, while taking a cut of any income they collect on your behalf.

Check it out at sentricmusic.com.

I have a publishing deal, but only for a few compositions specifically created for visual media. I haven't used Sentric, but that doesn't mean it isn't right for you.

Think carefully about how a publishing deal would help you at this time in your career.

Grand rights

Grand rights aren't something you need to deal with for self-releasing your music, but if you are involved in music for other stage-based dramatico-musical productions such as ballet, opera, or musical theatre, this is something to be aware of. Grand rights are negotiated on a case-by-case basis and aren't covered by PRS. For example, if you have written an opera and someone wants to stage it, you would negotiate a grand rights license that would likely be a cut of the box office ticket sales.

SUMMING UP, these are the organisations you should join, based on your role:

Your role	Organisation to join			
	PRS	MCPS	PPL (performer)	PPL (master rights holder)
Composer	✅	✅		
Performer			✅	
Record Label				✅

1. https://www.ppluk.com/membership/who-can-join-as-a-performer/
2. https://www.prsformusic.com/works/publisher-agreements

9

REGISTRATIONS, LICENCES, AND CODES

C hapter 8 was all about understanding your rights. This chapter is about how to register your work to ensure you collect money when those rights are exploited.

PRS and MCPS

Every time you write a composition, you need to fill out the registration form on the PRS/MCPS website, including any writing splits that you have agreed with various collaborators, including co-writers, songwriters, poets, or librettists. You agree how much each has given to the project and register that with PRS. For example, if you are in a four-person band and co-writing a song, you might agree each person is owed a 25% split of the composition. However, if someone has written the lyrics and been involved in developing the music, they might get 40% and the other three members get 20% each. Bands often fall out with each other over disagreements with writing splits, so you'll want to be very clear at the outset who is getting what percentage and why, have it written down and make sure everyone is happy. The Musicians' Union have an example contract available to members on their website. A link to which is on my resources page.

When you register works on the PRS website they will automatically appear on the MCPS database. Join MCPS if your music is released or about to be released. Royalties will be owed to you once your work is released and being listened to or when a physical product is created such as a CD. And remember that even if you join PRS to manage and administer mechanical rights, you still need to join MCPS separately.

MCPS and PRS have reciprocal agreements with other royalty collection services around the world, so if your music is used in different territories, you will still receive a royalty. It saves you having to register your music with each local PRO. During the registration process you will be asked to choose and register with any of the following American collection agencies: the American Society of Composers, Authors, and Publishers (ASCAP), Broadcast Music, Inc. (BMI), or the Society of European Stage Authors and Composers (SESAC). Each provides the same services, but you need to choose *one*.

AP2 licence. If you are releasing works by other composers or rights holders under your own label, you will need to contact MCPS to get an AP2 licence. You fill the AP2 license form with the information on the works you want to release and MCPS matches those works to their catalogue (and those of their international partners). They can then calculate how much royalty you will owe to the rights holders, and therefor how much the license will cost, based on the number of physical products you plan to release. In the UK, MCPS has a direct license with the streaming companies who report plays and pay a license fee to MCPS who then pay out to the rightsholders.

AP2 exclusion licence. If you are self-releasing your own work and plan to print CDs or other physical products, you need to contact MCPS for an *AP2 exclusion licence.* This licence confirms you own the work, and do not owe any royalties to a third party.

CD manufacturers will often ask to see either the AP2 licence or AP2 exclusion licence before printing CDs. This is to prove you have the legal right to create the CDs and you aren't asking the manufacturer to break copyright law. If you have any questions about the process, you can contact MCPS directly at https://www.prsformusic.com/help/contact-us.

International Standard Recording Code (ISRC)

Every recording released anywhere in the world has an **International Standard Recording Code (ISRC)**. An ISRC is an eleven-character alphanumeric code that identifies a specific recording and is unique to that recording. You need to create an ISRC for *each* recording, even if you are recording the same work multiple times, with the same underlying composition. For example, if you recorded and released three versions of '*Quartet No. 6*' by 'Matthew Whiteside', you would need to assign three different ISRCs, one to each recording, even though it is the same underlying composition.

When you join PPL as a Master Rights Holder, you will be given a five-character code (e.g., A2C4E) that is unique to you and forms the first part of the ISRC. Start with your five-letter code and add six numbers at the end to create your code:

- A2C4E 230001

You can use any numbers you want following your five-letter code, but the industry standard is to use this formula:

- [A2C4E] [YY] [RRRR]

Where Y = year, and R = recording number.

The recordings within one album might have ISRC codes that look like this:

- A2C4E 230001
- A2C4E 230002
- A2C4E 230003
- A2C4E 230004
- A2C4E 230005

These are the ISRCs for the first five recordings released by master rights holder A2C4E in the year 2023. This formula enables identification of the master rights holder, as well as easy discovery and retrieval of specific recordings. I highly recommend you create a spreadsheet which includes ISRCs for every recording you make along with other registration information. This additional information could be the PRS tune code which is PRS' unique identifier for each work registered with them, the ISWC (International Standard Musical Work Code) which is an internationally recognised reference number for the identification of musical works, the details who performed or worked on the recording or where it was recorded. Keep all information about all your recordings in one place. If someone wants to license your music for any reason you know exactly who was on the recording and how to contact them. It is also useful to refer to in case you forget someone's name or lose their contact details in your address book and want to work with them again.

Once you have created the ISRCs in your spreadsheet, you can register your recordings with PPL. During the registration process, you will be asked for other information such as track name, duration, performers, composers, recording location etc. As the record label, you are responsible for registering the performer details accurately to ensure they receive the royalties owed to them.

Registration could be very quick (string quartet) or very time consuming (80-player orchestra and 100-person chorus). Regardless, it is required. One of the pages within the registration process asks for the performer name, PPL ID, and instrument. If the musicians gave you their PPL ID number on the MU / BPI session form, type that into the search engine and the database should populate the performer's information for you. If they didn't give you their PPL ID, try searching for their name in the database, but if it doesn't exist, then just put their name and instrument on the form. PPL will match them to their PPL ID number if they are a member (or a member of an organisation with which PPL has a reciprocal agreement). If they aren't a member, PPL will hold their royalties for up to six years until they join.

There are two types of performer registration on each track: 'featured artist' and 'non-featured artist'. A 'featured artist' is the primary person or people performing on the recording. While the 'non-featured artist' is backing up the featured artist. For example, Taylor Swift would be a 'featured artist' while any backing singers or performers would be 'non-featured artist'. A string quartet would consist of four featured artists.

Once you have registered the individual tracks, you need to register the release. To do this, you need two additional numbers: the Universal Product Code and the catalogue number.

A digital distributor may offer to create ISRCs for you, but I recommend you create them yourself for three reasons:

1) If the information for the musicians hasn't been registered correctly, the musicians won't receive the royalties they are due.

2) The distributor would collect the income on your behalf and would take a cut for this service.

3) They sometimes charge you an administration fee to register on your behalf in addition to taking a cut of payments.

Universal Product Code

The **Universal Product Code (UPC)** is the barcode used to track sales across platforms and shops and used by the Official Charts Company to create the chart list. The UPC needs to be generated for you. Your distributor or sometimes the CD printing company can do this for you for a small fee. The UPC will also be used in your pre-save campaign which we will discuss in a later chapter.

Next, you will need to create the catalogue number, which is in alphanumeric format, for example: 'AB-0000'. (I used 'MW-0001' for my first release because 'Matthew Whiteside' is my label name.) The catalogue number is used as an internal reference for your own record label filing purposes. This can be tedious but must be done (PPL has good guidance on their website if you need help).

Once you've generated the ISRCs, you can amend your PRS registration to include them. This isn't required, but it is good practice to ensure royalties are allocated accurately. The PPL and PRS/MCPS systems are gradually sharing more information with each other. If one system knows about a recording being broadcast and the other doesn't, they will talk to each other so the one that hasn't been paid will chase the relevant company to pay the royalties. It is a bit more complicated than that but that's the simplified explanation.

Gesellschaft für Verwertung von Leistungsschutzrechte (GVL) label code

As master rights holder, you will need to request a **Gesellschaft für Verwertung von Leistungsschutzrechte (GVL)** label code. GVL is the German version of PPL. This code makes it easier to track and collect royalties in Germany. Make sure you get it when you register with PPL.

Organising recording information

At this point in the chapter, you might be overwhelmed thinking about all the coding and registration information you need to log for each recording. I use the table below to organise the data for my music catalogue.

Album Name	UPC	Catalogue Number	ISRC	Track Name	Track Duration	Player Name	Player PPL ID
Album One	123456789111	MW-0001	A2C4E 230001	Me Thinks	03:23	John Doe	1104018477
		MW-0001	A2C4E 230001	Me Thinks	03:23	Jane Doe	2204022477
		MW-0001	A2C4E 230002	Another Sonata	15:25	Jane Doe	2204022477
		MW-0001	A2C4E 230003	The World in an Oyster	05:54	Sarah Curtis	7774018237
Album Two	123456789999	MW-0002	A2C4E 230004	Two Step	01:29	Jo Smith	6384013237
		MW-0002	A2C4E 230005	Hells Violin	23:12	John Doe	1104018477
		MW-0002	A2C4E 230006	Everything Now	03:21	John Doe	1104018477

Spreadsheet for organising recording information

CHECKLIST:

- Register with PPL
- Get your ISRC start code
- Get your label code or GVL code
- Generate complete ISRCs for each release
- Get UPC from distributor
- Complete PPL recording and release registrations
- Create a system for logging information for each of your recordings

10

CHOOSING A DISTRIBUTOR

A s an independent entity, you have access to many distributors. Each one will offer slightly different deals and often change their deals over time. How do you know which one to choose? I have provided examples from three of the most popular to give you a sense of the terms they offer. I am not pushing you to sign with any of these distributors, but since most people are familiar with these brands, I thought these examples would be the most helpful. CD Baby and TuneCore have similar terms and cover everything offered from other providers. Bandcamp, however, is altogether different in how it operates.

How different distributors work

CD Baby

CD Baby charge a flat fee and a percentage of royalties, 9% of downloads and streaming and 30% of YouTube, Facebook, and Instagram. They also have an option called 'pro-tier' that offers global royalty collection and global song registration. However, if you are a member of MCPS and PRS, or your local equivalent PRO, you can ignore the pro-tier option, as you will already be covered.

Single of $9.95 and for an album of $29

Pro-tier: $24.99 for a single and $69 for an album.

TUNECORE

TuneCore offer pay-per-release and unlimited plans.

Pay-per-release has no upfront costs, but they take 20% of your income. You could opt for a subscription of $9.99 per year for a single and $29.99 per year for an album. But with these subscriptions you keep all your digital revenue.

The Unlimited Plans are $14.99, $29.99, and $49.99 per year for unlimited releases. Each price point gives a different level of service, but each level allocates 100% of your royalties to you.

Your options are:

- an upfront fee with a percentage cut, but your music is available indefinitely
- no upfront fee with a higher percentage cut, but your music is available indefinitely
- a subscription-based model with no percentage cut, but when you stop paying, your music is taken down

You need to decide what will bring the most value to your business in the long term. For example, if you think you are going to earn £50 a year, the best option might be no upfront fee with a percentage cut. If you think you are going to earn £5000+ a year, a subscription would be better. From my experience, most streams and sales take place on the release date and the year or so after, because of the marketing you have done to promote your music. You won't want to pay subscription fees for dwindling sales five years down the line. You could release your music on a subscription-based model for the first year or two and then move over to an upfront fee model after that. However, moving your release can be frustrating and could confuse royalty payment flow.

Both models are good, and you will need to decide which is best for your business.

BANDCAMP

Bandcamp distributes only on its own platform. This distinguishes it from distributors like CD Baby and TuneCore. Bandcamp allows you to sell digital downloads, physical audio products, merchandise, scores, etc. through their online store. You can even set up your own subscription streaming service which would allow people, for a fee, to listen to your music. Bandcamp doesn't charge for using their services or for setting up an artist's site. You can set your own price on your products which you can't do anywhere else. Their earnings come from 15% of digital sales and 10% of physical sales.

Bandcamp has a reputation for being supportive of independent artists through schemes like their Bandcamp Fridays and their in-house promotional and review teams. In addition, customers who buy music from Bandcamp know they are purchasing directly from the people who are making the music, and they often choose to pay more than the price you've set. I find it happens more times than not, and it's always such a lovely, supportive gesture.

OTHER OPTIONS

If you want to go with a classical specialist streaming company such as Idagio or Naxos, you will need to distribute through a company called FUGA, who happen to own CD Baby. You could also work with distributors like the Orchard or Independent Digital who are application-based and very selective when choosing the labels they work with. They prefer dealing with larger catalogues and can provide services such as playlist pitching. If you are just starting out, these options (FUGA, the Orchard, or Independent Digital) might be too expensive, take too large a cut of your income, or require that you fill out an application before they would even consider distributing your music. As an independent releasing artist, I recommend that you pursue the mainstream non-curating distributors like CD Baby, TuneCore, Emu Bands, Route Note, Distro Kid, and others.

All distributors (except for Bandcamp) will send your music to the main platforms: Spotify, Apple Music, Deezer, Amazon and Tidal. Some of them have more options when it comes to distribution outside of Europe and America, but broadly, they are comparable. Always distribute through Bandcamp in addition to *one* other digital distributor (such as CD Baby or TuneCore). This will give you the widest possible coverage for your music. If you use more than one distributor to get your music onto streaming platforms, it will confuse the flow of royalties and you might not get anything.

The distribution process

This book focuses on digital distribution, but audiences also like to have physical copies of CDs. In the past, the only way they could buy physical copies was by going to a shop. These days there are very few brick-and-mortar shops that sell CDs. Even the ones that do are unlikely to stock an independent release by an unknown artist. So how do you get your physical CDs to your fans?

As mentioned earlier in this chapter, you can sell your CDs through Bandcamp. You can also sell CDs at your live performances or through your own website. I suggest you sign up to Sumup, Zettle, or similar. These are services that allow you to take card payments in person. After the purchase, the card reader service provider takes a percentage of every transaction that goes through them. As we are very close to a cashless society, having the ability to take card payments in person is very important.

Another option is Amazon. Amazon has the greatest reach and distribution network of any company in the world. Many of the listings you see on Amazon are not actually sold by Amazon. Instead, Amazon acts as a front end, customer-discovery mechanism for tens of thousands of independent sellers. It is easy to add yourself to this list.

Go to www.sell.amazon.co.uk and sign up for a

merchant account. From there you can set up your own shop on Amazon. You can choose to fulfil sales yourself or send copies to Amazon's warehouse so they can fulfil sales on your behalf and customers can get next day delivery through Prime.

Regardless of the distribution method you choose, all distributors will ask for the following information:

1. track name
2. artist(s) name(s) (with classical music, this will also be the composer)
3. ISRC
4. composer (and publisher, if relevant)
5. record label name
6. audio files
7. artwork/design files

We've already discussed items 1-4. Let's look at what you need to consider with record label name, audio files, and artwork.

RECORD LABEL NAME. Your record label name is your marketing brand. I use my name, *Matthew Whiteside*, for my record label. I created *TNW Music* as the record label of my concert production company, *The Night With...* I wanted to differentiate the releases of *The Night With...* from the concerts by using different brands, though they are owned by the same company. Your record label name is a way to build your market identity.

· · ·

AUDIO FILES. Make sure you and the mastering engineer know in what format your distributor wants the audio files. Once you determine that no more changes will be made to your recording and it is in the correct format for your distributor, your recording is considered finalised. Upload the audio files to the distributor and agree a **release date**, the specific date for when your music will be available for sale through the distributor. This is usually a minimum of 3 months from the time you send the finalised files. For example, if you finalise the release on March 1, you should be aiming for a June 1 release *at the earliest* to allow time to develop and launch your marketing strategy. During this 3-month period you would put all your efforts into publicising the recording. If you delayed promoting your release, your efforts would likely have little to no impact on the success of your launch. Also, make sure the day you choose to release is a Friday. This is the industry standard day to release music and when all the new music playlists get updated.

ARTWORK FILES. As with the audio files, you and your designer need to know which format your distributor wants you to use for the artwork before uploading the files. As for the artwork itself, we will cover this in the next chapter: Design and Branding.

11

DESIGN, BRANDING, AND PRINTING

W e all know the adage, 'Don't judge a book by its cover'. We humans are visual creatures and judge everything based on first impressions–in fact, in the first seven seconds.[1] The music market is flooded with products. How can yours be instantly eye-catching in an era of visual saturation?

Cover design

What are you trying to communicate through your music? Your cover design should communicate the same thing. A cover design will include artwork, text fonts, layout, marketing blurbs or other elements regardless of product format (CD, vinyl, streaming).

Most albums feature a photo, painting, sculpture, graphic or other artwork on their covers. A cover designer would design the front and back covers, insert, and lyric sheet (if relevant). You can choose whatever elements you want if the design meets the formatting and content guidelines of your distributor, printing company, and publisher. A professional cover designer will ensure this is done properly. If you are only planning a digital release, you only need to think of the cover. Head to my website www.matthewwhiteside.co.uk/guidebook-resources to see full colour examples of everything I'm about to discuss.

When planning your cover art, you need to think about whether you want to follow the genre norm or do something different. The typical album cover for string quartets features everyone wearing black holding their instruments. You could stay within that norm or do something to distinguish yourself in a crowded market.

For example, Diamanda La Berge Dramm's album, *Inside Out*, uses a striking portrait of the performer that doesn't suggest the album contains Bach. In another example, contemporary composer, Caroline Shaw, opted for album covers that departed from the norm. She chose images that conveyed the content of her music and made her stand out from other composers. Her covers have a consistent look and feel that support her brand. Look at the covers and explore her music on her website: www.carolineshaw.com. You'll get a sense of what I mean.

There isn't a right or wrong approach to cover design–just one that is right for you, your music, and your brand.

You could sketch the cover art yourself, use a stock image, hire a professional photographer, or commission an artist to create a graphic inspired by your music. Your designer might also be able to create the artwork, which would streamline the process considerably. Whatever you choose, budget for it, and make sure you obtain permission to use it for the marketing and release of the album. If you are commissioning someone to create your cover image, that can simply be written into your contract with them. If you are trying to license an already existing image, you will need to contact the agency or individual and request and pay for the permission to use it.

Cover art of my first album Dichroic Light by
Dominika Mayovich

The artwork for all my album covers have been created by Dominika Mayovich. We started collaborating in 2014 for a sound/art installation and for the cover of *Dichroic Light*. I send her the recording masters and ask her to create an image in response to the music. Next, she sends me some sketches, and I make some comments. Lastly, she either sends me revised sketches, incorporating my comments, or she creates the final work. This collaborative way of working ensures that the covers will accurately represent the music (and I get artwork that looks beautiful on the walls!). She is also a tattoo artist! Check out her work at www.mayovich.com or her tattoos on Instagram @mayovichink.

I also work with www.hlavi.com to do the text design and layout. He has created many of the covers for TNW Music releases and the cover of this book.

Branding

A **brand** refers to a product's identity and how it is perceived in a market. A successful brand will create awareness of a product and establish a connection with your target audience before any products are even available. For example, Apple and Microsoft are two tech companies that sell computers, software, and other devices, but each brand evokes specific images and emotions. For me, Apple means good–if a little pricy–computers, excellent and intuitive user interface and joined-up devices. On the other hand (for me), Microsoft means cheap feeling computers and frustrating connectivity. I associate most people using Microsoft-based computers as having desk jobs. If I'm looking for another computer, I would never contemplate buying one powered by Microsoft software–not just because I don't like the hardware, but because 'I am not that kind of person'. It's no longer about the product per se; it's about how I define myself as a person. Though, some of the software I use only works on Mac. So, it isn't just about brand loyalty. You may feel the exact opposite about Apple and Microsoft products. But this is the power of a brand. These companies spend billions on building their brands to secure your business and your loyalty.

Think of Brian Blessed, Steve Jobs, or Taylor Swift. Each of these people evokes a specific image that is familiar to us. We can feel like we know these celebrities, but we don't, we only know their projected brand. This is the same with politicians, TV presenters, sports teams, film stars, and anyone or anything else in the public eye.

A brand is an empty vessel that meaning is poured into to support its desired aim – sales, influence, money, votes.

Musicians' brands are supported by websites, head-shots, music videos, and social media posts that communicate a consistent message to the targeted audience. Many bands often have a logo that they can hang their band's brand on as a visual identifier, in the same way that Apple does. When I see *Disturbed's* logo, I recognise it instantly and can hear any number of their songs in my head. Or Iron Maiden's Eddie mascot. Mascots are just another way to signify a brand. You likely have had the same experience with other bands.

All the large music companies have a distinct visual identity. Both Deutsche Gramophone's yellow banner and Naxos' white surround with image and text are instantly recognisable. Those branding images are associated with a specific type of music. The same applies to music publishers. Peters Edition and Faber have distinct logos that instantly identify the kind of composers Peters and Faber represent. Check out examples of these on my website at www.matthewwhiteside.co.uk/guidebook-resources.

The most important component for leveraging the power of branding is consistency. I've used the same designer for all my cover artwork, so my releases have a consistent look and feel. People make the connection between the artwork and my brand. I also have a logo (see below) which I have on my business card, website, scores, the physical CDs, and the cover of this book. I quite enjoy that my initials are an ambigram.

My brand is my name – Matthew Whiteside. And my name means different things and possibilities to different people. To some people, my brand signifies the style of my music and the emotions it conjures when they listen to it. To others it is the possibility of a performance or a commission as part of my work for *The Night With...* or it represents my teaching and mentoring activities (of which this book is part). A brand can mean multiple things to multiple people. Understanding how people see your brand can help you grow your business. It can also help you understand how different parts of your business can support the other parts. This is veering into marketing which I'll talk about later.

How does all this talk of branding link to your release? Your cover design will be the most important visual asset you have for your release. It will be used throughout your marketing and advertising campaigns, on your website, in your emails, through your distributor and through social media. You want to use the same image consistently so that every time someone sees it, they think of your music. I'll talk a bit more about this later in the marketing section. Branding and marketing go hand in hand, but they are separate things to consider.

Another thing to consider about branding is how you physically appear and act in the world. I was recently talking to an indie rock musician who was complaining about how people kept being surprised by her music when they heard it and making unwanted suggestions about the kind of music she should perform or cover. The main reason for this was how she presented herself to the world. She looks like Dolly Parton, but her music is indie rock, like *Royal Blood*, rather than Dolly Parton's country sound. This confused people when they heard her music – the image she projected suggested a different genre than what they were hearing. This artist hadn't realised the clothes she wore primed people to think of a specific sound because of Dolly Parton's well-known brand. This is an example of someone else's brand affecting yours. Never present yourself in a way that makes you uncomfortable but do be aware of how your appearance affects your brand and how it could influence your potential following. Be aware of the norms of your genre and make an active choice to work within or against them.

If you want to explore this more, the overarching field of study for is called 'semiotics'. It is a fascinating and confusing topic to explore. When I read Italio Calvin's book, *Invisible Cities*, it helped me understand and internalise semiotics and its wider ramifications. The idea is that a symbol signifies something, but isn't the thing itself. For example, a barber's red, white and blue pole signifies there is a barber, but the pole is not the barber.

The more you think of your brand and what it signifies, the more you will start thinking of yourself as the business that you are. By releasing your music, you are promoting your brand. And the more people see it, the more inclined they will be to buy your product. You may even get to a point where your brand signifies something else, priming people on how to perceive other brands.

What brand identity do you want to evoke? What do you want listeners, fans, and potential clients to think of when they hear your name or see your image?

Printing

Assuming you want a printed product (e.g., a CD) to support your brand and sell at concerts, you will need to find a printing company. If you have your UPC (barcode), the GVL (aka, the label code), any text or liner notes, and the standard copyright notice, you can finalise the design of your CD and send it for printing. Make sure your designer knows what template the printer uses–they all use different ones. If you use the wrong one it could delay your release, compromise your marketing strategy, and ultimately, the perception of your music and your brand. Avoid this by hiring an experienced professional designer.

Ask the printer for their turnaround time, as it will determine your release date and promotional activities. I usually leave four weeks to get the printed CDs, but I've had them as fast as five days and as slow as ten weeks.

If you want to release your music on vinyl, you will have to wait a lot longer, sometimes years! One vinyl pressing plant I spoke to quoted an 8-month turnaround time if you booked in a project with them today. The reason for this is because of the increased demand for vinyl releases. The production capacity hasn't increased with demand. Setting up a vinyl pressing plant is expensive. Seabass Vinyl is expected to open in 2023 in Scotland so that should help reduce wait times back to the 8-12 weeks that was being quoted pre-pandemic. I'd suggest if you want to release on vinyl, do it as a second release for your super fans or collectors after the main release of the album. It could be a good second marketing opportunity to get more press interest. You could even do it as a limited-edition pre-order so you don't print too many and waste your money. Vinyl isn't cheap.

On my website is an example of a CD printing template supplied by BirnamCD, the company I use, to print all my and TNW Music's physical CDs. You can see an example of a completed template so you get an idea of how it should be filled in. However, Birnam also have a helpful guide on how to work with this template on their website. Make sure you read their instructions and their guide.

---

1. https://www.scienceofpeople.com/first-impressions/

PUBLIC RELATIONS

Y ou are at the point where your music is digitally flying its way to streaming companies' databases, you have everything registered with PRS, MCPS and PPL, and you might even have some physical CDs waiting to be sent out into the world. Your beautiful music is ready to be released! You want to shout about it and get it into listeners' ears. But hold off a little, you need to come up with a strategy for how to do this effectively. This is where public relations will help.

Public relations (PR) firms and freelancers are responsible for working with you to shape a positive, public-facing brand and to frame your music, so it is 'heard' by your intended audience. A PR specialist will pitch your product to journalists, radio stations, and other organizations who in turn will sell your product to their audiences– a type of business-to-business (B2B) model. Remember, you are a business.

Sometimes PR specialists are called 'pluggers'. This is a more informal term, but they do the same thing, promoting you and your music. I'll use the term, PR, for the rest of this chapter but be aware that PR and plugging are interchangeable terms.

Finding a PR provider

Are there any PR campaigns for a similar project that impressed you? What specifically impressed you about the campaign? Ask your connections who they would recommend or Google. There isn't a central database of PR providers and even if there were, each of them has a different specialty area. Here are a few of the things I look for in a PR provider:

- Previous clients: Are they like me? For example, if the PR group only works with rap artists, they are unlikely to have the right connections to help your release of 12th century plainsong.
- Coverage: What have they done for previous clients? You can either request this directly or do a bit of digging on your own. Search for the release the provider worked on and find any press coverage.
- Cost: Can you afford them? Remember that quotes from larger companies will add VAT which will be 20% more expensive.

Once you've contacted a PR provider, the firm or individual will set up an appointment with you to get to know you, your music, and your goals, and to determine if it's a good fit. PR people often have specialty areas, and if they aren't right for you and your music, they will refer you to someone else.

As soon as you've found a person or company you want to work with, ask for a quote. If possible, do your due-diligence and get quotes from at least three different PR providers. This will put you in a better negotiating position. Keep in mind that no PR provider can guarantee anything. They can't guarantee you coverage, sales, playlist placement, or income, regardless of how experienced or well-connected they might be. If they do make this claim, they are naïve, aren't being entirely truthful, or they are promising services that aren't worth having (e.g., a playlist placement that is simply listened to by bots).

PR can cost as much as you can afford, anywhere from the thousands up to the tens of thousands, and well beyond depending on the scope (local, national, international) and duration of the campaign. If you are relying on funding, you may need to revise your promotional strategy depending on the amount of funding you receive. For example, if your funding is less than what you had anticipated, your PR person may be willing to provide the same services at a lower cost or they may have to scale back on the strategy. The campaign you had originally envisioned that covered the UK and Ireland may now only allow you to cover the UK.

Once you've agreed on the scope of work, the PR specialist will issue a contract outlining the fee, specific services, duration of services, periodical or geographical targets, reporting, or any other terms you have discussed.

Working with your PR provider

Release strategy. After the contract is signed, the PR provider will start working with you to develop the **release strategy**, the master plan that follows a timeline for the successful release of your music. A release strategy incorporates public relations and marketing, takes dedicated time to plan and develop, and could have the single biggest impact on getting your music known. Remember that you need to set a release date (the date your music is made available for sale) a *minimum* of three months from the day you send the final release to the distributor to give you time to create your release strategy. If you are working another job or have many projects on the go, you might need to have a bit more lead time than three months to allow yourself breathing space. However, don't give yourself too much time or you might fall fowl of Parkinson's Law, the adage that any work will expand to fill the time allotted for its completion. It's why I find deadlines handy even if they do occasionally whiz by.

SHAPING YOUR STORY. A **story** is the narrative PR providers create to frame you and your work to engage both the media and potential customers. You may have more than one story to tell. Maybe you are collaborating with a craftsman who makes ceramic instruments, or with a local historian whose research has uncovered tales you've set to music. These stories could reach a broader audience, appealing to niche interest groups and even to people outside of the music business. One of the most interesting extra-musical things I've been involved in was when I was commissioned by the Institute of Physics to write my *Quartet No. 4 (Entangled)*, a piece based on quantum physics. My 2019 album, *Entangled*, featured this work which was a large part of the story of the release and influenced the album artwork. The CD even features imagery of quantum entanglement published in 2019. This extra-musical influence allowed me to reach a larger audience than I would have if I had only marketed to those interested in contemporary music.

GATHERING YOUR ASSETS. Prior to release, your public relations provider will be contacting journalists and media outlets, and you will be building your presence on social media. These activities require you to have assets you can use for promoting your work, including album artwork, reviews or blurbs, photos from the recording sessions, photos from live performances (composer in front of ensemble bowing is a standard for composers of you singing into a microphone in front of a large crowd if you are a singer) or your headshots/press photos (or all of these!). Your assets need to be consistent with the brand you are trying to create. Remember to include the cost of a professional photoshoot in the overall project budget. An album release is a great time to refresh your photos.

ASSEMBLING AND MAILING YOUR PRESS KIT. After your PR provider has finalised the strategy, they will put together a press release or info sheet. A copy of my press kit for

Entangled is on my website at www.matthewwhiteside.-
co.uk/guidebook-resources. (You can use extracts of the
press pack in your social media, too.) The PR firm will
send the press kit to their contacts, introducing you and
following up to secure commitments to get you, your
music, and your story featured in reviews, previews, articles, magazine, and blog content. Although they can't
strong-arm their contacts, a good PR person will pester
their contacts in the nicest possible way to convince them
to include you!

The press kit will include:

- the press release or info sheet for the release
- cover art for the album
- promo shots of you
- streaming links (these might be private at this
  point)
- link to a music video (if you have made one)

Ideally, you would host your press kit on your website
or on your cloud drive so it can be easily shared and
downloaded by journalists.

REGULAR REPORTING. Your PR provider should give you
regular reports on the work they have done on your
behalf (make sure this is in your contract!). These reports
could be monthly or weekly and will include an end-of-
relationship report summarising the coverage they have
given you. You would include this report in your end-of-
project reporting for your funder so they can see some

measurable results of their investment. You can also use these reports in ads and other promotional activities to build excitement and anticipation prior to release. You can also use these reports in a more live way for example use press quotes, that are highlighted within the report, a new advert that you create or target an advert at a publication's YouTube channel. I'll talk more about that in the next chapter on marketing.

TIMING IS EVERYTHING. Let's say a magazine has just completed an article on recorder quartets that will be published in two months. Music for recorder quartets is your specialty and is the focus of your latest release. You were late hiring someone to do your PR. Your PR person contacts the magazine and pitches you and your work to them. The magazine just devoted an issue to recorder quartets, so they won't be featuring you any time soon. If you had contacted them just one month earlier, you would have had a much higher chance of being included. It's important to plan well ahead of time to make the most of your opportunities (and your PR budget!). Your PR person should know about the magazine's content plans for the next several months and be able to advise you accordingly. A good PR specialist will have regular meetings with the relevant magazines and other periodicals to share their goals and slates of work. PR specialists and magazines have a symbiotic relationship, so it is critical that they have regular open and trusting communications.

13

MARKETING AND ADVERTISING

As you learned in the previous chapter, public relations focus on developing and sustaining a positive image of a brand or person through free channels, such as reviews, blogs, and articles. **Marketing** focuses on gathering market data to define, target and develop customers and products. A **marketing campaign** defines the specific activities undertaken over a given period to engage the target audience; for example, buying advertising space on paid-for channels such as Facebook, Instagram, Google, TikTok, X / Twitter, and Spotify. Sometimes, a PR company can create your marketing campaign for an additional fee.

ADVERTISING IS a marketing activity that communicates product information to the customer in a compelling way. When it comes to advertising, you want to look at where you'll get the biggest return on investment. Spotify might seem like an ideal place to advertise, but the minimum spend is high. Moreover, Spotify target people who are on the free, ad-supported tier with the lowest value streams. To me, it doesn't seem like a good investment to target people who won't or can't pay for music. Billboard and print advertising are an option, but in my experience, they are very costly and don't bring enough value for the cost. Similarly, X / Twitter is expensive for what you get in return. In this next section, I will focus on Facebook/Instagram (Meta) and Google because they are the advertising channels with which I have had the most experience and success. I will also touch on influencer marketing.

Let's start with the most important aspect of marketing and advertising: the customer journey.

The customer journey

The **customer journey** refers to the steps a customer goes through leading up to a purchase and staying loyal to a brand. A customer becomes aware of your music, engages with it, buys it, and searches for more. If you craft your marketing campaign to support each part of the customer journey, you will have greater chances of creating a loyal base of users.

Marketing funnel

A **marketing funnel** is a concept used in marketing campaigns to map out the customer journey and understand what you want them to do at each stage. The funnel shape represents how at the beginning of a campaign you want to cast a very wide net to capture as many leads as possible (see Figure 13.1). As potential customers progress through the subsequent stages, fewer customers will stay with the brand and carry on with the journey to the next level. Customer loyalty is developed by giving the customer something they want or need at different stages in the journey to keep them engaged, both before and after they make a purchase or perform an action that you find valuable like pre-saving your music or joining your mailing list. There are six stages in a marketing funnel:

1. Awareness Stage

The aim of this stage is to generate curiosity and excitement about your music and the upcoming release. You want to build anticipation for the release through:

- **Social Media Teasers:** Share these teaser videos on platforms like Instagram, Facebook, and X / Twitter.
- **Countdown Campaign:** Start a countdown campaign on social media, building anticipation for the album's release date.
- **Teaser Videos:** Create short teaser videos or trailers that provide a sneak peek of the upcoming album, featuring snippets of the music and visuals (maybe a close-up of a detail in the album art).

2. Interest Stage

Building on the awareness stage, provide more in-depth insights into the album's creation and your creative journey. You want to encourage your listeners (or potential listeners) to get excited and to be drawn further into the story through:

- **Behind-the-Scenes Insights:** Share behind-the-scenes videos or posts that offer insights into the album's creation process, studio sessions, and inspirations.
- **Single Releases:** Release one or more singles from the album with accompanying music video (if you have one).
- **Album Cover Reveal:** Unveil the album cover design and explain the concept or symbolism behind it.

3. Consideration Stage

This is where you need to convince your audience that the album offers something that is worth their attention and support:

- **Album Preview:** Provide an extended preview of the album, showcasing snippets from each track and discussing the overarching theme or narrative. Maybe this could be offered to a blog as a pre-view article.
- **Exclusive Content:** Offer exclusive content such as acoustic versions, demo recordings, or alternate takes for those who pre-order or sign up.
- **Collaboration Stories:** Share stories about any collaborations or guest appearances on the album, highlighting the unique elements.

- **Press Quotes:** preview press coverage should be starting around this stage of the release which you should be sharing to support why your music is worth listening to.

4. Intent Stage

This stage is where you convert interested fans into pre-order customers by offering exclusive perks, such as:

- **Pre-Order and Pre-Save Campaign:** Launch a pre-order and pre-save campaign with special incentives like limited edition merchandise, signed copies, or early access to the full album.
- **Track-by-Track Breakdown:** Provide in-depth insights into each track, discussing its inspiration, composition, and significance within the album.

5. Purchase Stage

You want to make sure the interest you have built converts into people buying and streaming your music. An effective way to do this is to mark the release with a celebratory atmosphere on your social media. Here are some ideas:

- **Release Day Celebrations:** Launch the album with a dedicated online event, live stream, or virtual release party.
- **Digital and Physical Distribution:** Make the album available for purchase and streaming on

various platforms, and ensure physical copies are readily accessible.

- **Thank You Messages:** Express gratitude to your fans and supporters for their role in making the album a reality.

6. Loyalty Stage

The release is just the beginning of the story. You want to build loyal fans who will return to your music and keep supporting you. This requires fostering long-term connections with them. The album is just the start. Here are ways to build an ongoing relationship with fans:

- **Behind-the-Scenes Insights:** Continue sharing insights and stories related to the album's reception, reviews, and fan reactions.
- **Interactive Challenges:** Create challenges or contests that encourage fans to engage with the album creatively, such as cover song contests or art competitions.
- **Limited-Time Offers:** Provide exclusive discounts or bundles for those who purchased the album, encouraging them to share their experience with others.
- **Keep Sharing:** Share stories about performances, press reviews or radio play to keep the music and you in audiences' minds.
- **Free Things:** You could offer a free track to people who sign up to your mailing list or, as I

do, a discount code useable on anything for sale on my website or Bandcamp including scores, albums, or this book. Incidentally, you can sign up to my mailing list here http://eepurl.com/dy0IcL.

But Stage 6 isn't the end! You will have to repeat each step in the funnel to expand your target audience and to keep building a deeper interest and loyalty to you, your music, and your activities.

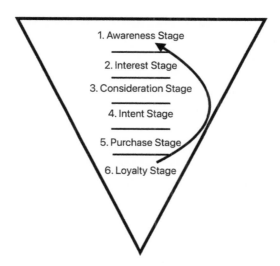

Figure 13.1 Marketing Funnel

The 'Rule of Seven'

The 'Rule of Seven'[1] is a marketing concept that was developed in the early 1900's that says a consumer needs to have seven points of contact with a product before they will make a purchase. These points of contact could be paid-for ads on Meta or Google; they could be PR-based blurbs, such as a reviewer saying, 'This album is great, buy it'; it could be word-of-mouth from friends praising your work; it could be through your social media posts and your mailing list. While the internet has made it much easier for people to shout about their work, this rule of seven is still a good way to think about marketing. How can you get someone to see a mention of your release seven times without it seeming repetitive and boring? Keep this in mind as we highlight different ways to promote your music and when you are creating your assets.

Defining your target audience using different platforms

META

Interest buckets. Meta, the parent company of Facebook and Instagram, use demographic and interest-based data to create a target audience. When you build your ad through their platform, Meta will ask you to define the location, age, and gender of your target audience. You will be asked to choose **interest buckets**; that is, users of Facebook and Instagram who, based on data gathered from the platforms, are grouped and marketed to according to their shared interests. Interest buckets will include general categories like string quartets, classical music, rock music, BBC Radio 2, BBC Radio 3 etc, and sometimes include specific categories like individual composers. These interest buckets are constantly changing based on the ongoing data collection of Meta. (I've searched for buckets that I used in the past only to find they're not there the next time I run a campaign.)

You will have options to narrow the search further for these buckets by using 'and' or 'exclude' with additional criteria. For example, you might want to set up an advertising audience for people:

- in the UK
- between 30 and 60
- interested in classical music
- **and** who are interested in Spotify

This would be good targeting for an advert that included the text, 'stream on Spotify now'. Likewise change the 'interested in Spotify' to 'interested in Apple Music' for Apple Music.

You can add as many narrowing clauses as you want, but don't go too narrow or your ad might not reach anyone. Though sometimes you might want to go very narrow to try and target an advert at attendees of a specific event – for example a music festival or a conference. You could be showcasing your work at WOMEX so you could run an advert targeting a 2km radius around the venue targeted at people who are interested in the kind of music you perform.

The interface to set up an ad on both Facebook and/or Instagram is the same and is intuitive; the true skill is setting up the defining data as accurately as possible to target the right people. You might want to change the buckets and assets and set up multiple ads and test them to see what works most effectively. The reach and engagement of the ad can be tracked through Meta's advertising interface. These metrics change depending on the aim of your ad but include things like 'Link Clicks', 'Cost per Link Click' (lower is better!), 'Page Likes', 'Reach' (how many individuals saw the ad), and 'Impressions' (how many times that ad was shown to people). If you divide 'Impressions' by 'Reach' that will tell you how many times a single user saw the ad.

These buckets are not just music specific. They cover every conceivable topic someone might want to market on Meta. For my 2019 release, *Entangled*, I created an ad targeting scientists and those involved in quantum physics hoping it might grab their interest enough to listen to my music.

PRE-DEFINED AUDIENCES. You can ask Meta to build an audience that 'looks like' (in data terms) a pre-defined audience. This lookalike audience can then be used as the target audience for your advertising, enabling you to reach people who are not yet familiar with your work but are likely to be interested in it. This audience would be derived from people who follow your page on Facebook or Instagram, have seen a post of yours but don't follow you, have watched a certain percentage of a video you've posted, or have visited your website. How does Meta know if someone has visited your website? Through their Pixel.

. . .

THE META PIXEL. Meta's platform will track your website traffic through the Meta Pixel. This is code that you install in your website to feed data to Meta. Meta will match people's profile with the data that is sent from the Pixel. This is why you start seeing ads appear on your social media feed for a website you recently visited. That website has a pixel installed.

The Meta Pixel can also be used for re-targeting. Re-targeting is when you create an ad for people who have been on your website, and you want to remind them that you exist. It will also target people who have added something to their basket on your website but have not yet followed through with the purchase. You can run campaigns targeting all these people with different messages. For example, you could run a campaign that includes a discount code aimed at people who have added something to their basket but have not yet purchased it to encourage them to complete the order. The Pixel is a powerful way to develop and engage your audience and to reach new people! If you install the Pixel, make sure to update your GDPR statement on your website to inform visitors.

CREATING AN ADVERTISEMENT. Your advertisement will be a combination of text and image, or text and video that Meta will show across their platforms and partners. Earlier I discussed the importance of creating advertising assets with photos, videos, and artwork. One of the most effective advertising assets I had for *Entangled* was a photo of me in the studio in front of the Aurea Quartet. It was a selfie; it was slightly silly, but people engaged with it (see Figure 13.2).

Figure 13.2 Me and the Aurea Quartet (Julian Azkoul, Rosemary Attree, Christine Anderson, and Abby Hayward). Make sure you budget for photos in your recording session.

Meta favours video: it prioritises video content over static images, so make sure you have at least one video that incorporates your music to use as an advertising asset. Meta also allows you to create videos from images you upload to their platform.

Meta has their own information pages on the advertising tools they have and how to use them. They are quite extensive but very useful to dive into if you want to advertise on their platform. Check out the information here: www.facebook.com/business/tools/ads-manager but there are also links to other guides on my website. And yes, I do have a pixel installed.

There are two reasons for hosting content on my website for you to read through this book – the main one is image quality. A lot of the images I am sharing aren't going to print well, without doubling the cost of the book, so I'm hosting them on my website. The other reason is to help me market this book. If you have read this book and engaged with it enough to head to my website for more information, I can safely assume someone else like you will be interested in this book. I will be using the data to market to new people to help them establish and develop their career in music. I wanted to be open about that to model how to think creatively to leverage your product, and also show you that these tools aren't music specific.

Google

Google advertising options are like those for Facebook/Instagram, but in my opinion, less intuitive to use. Google can retarget people in the same way as Meta through Google Analytics. However, Google bases their targeting on words that people use they when search for something. When you are creating your target audience in Google, you set up keywords that people may be searching for. If someone types in the keyword or phrase that matches your ad, and you 'win the auction', your ad will appear at the top of the search results page. Likewise, if your keywords or phrases appear on or within a website, your ad will appear as one of the ads to be displayed on that website.

'Win the auction' refers to the way digital ads are sold (both Google and Meta use this system). There is a behind-the-scenes 'auction' every time a webpage requests an ad. If your ad aligns most closely with the interests of the website's target audience, you win and get displayed. These auctions and how they work are closely guarded secrets, but they allow for democratisation of advertising across the internet–not just ads from massive companies (like with TV advertising), but from smaller independent creators or shops. You can get your product or service in front of many people for a few hundred pounds rather than for tens of thousands of pounds. It means you can get your new string quartet in front of people who might want to listen to it or a book you are self-publishing on self-releasing to musicians trying to take their first steps in releasing their own music.

If you were advertising a new album of string quartet music that features your music and Kaija Saariaho, I would choose keywords/phrases like:

- String quartet
- Contemporary string quartet
- Contemporary classical
- New string quartet
- Kaija Saariaho
- Kaija Saariaho [piece name]
- [your name]
- [players' names]
- [quartet's name]

These are starting points. Google will also suggest other keywords linked to ones you have suggested.

While Google's keyword method might not be the best for targeting potential new listeners, it can be an effective way to sell tickets (and help with the Rule of Seven). For example, people who are searching for 'classical concerts in May in Edinburgh' would likely find tickets for your ensemble's performance in Usher Hall on May 25th.

Google is the parent company of YouTube, and YouTube outshines all other platforms in its ability to target specific audiences when it comes to music.

YouTube

The pre-roll ads on YouTube can be very annoying when all you want to do is watch the video you just searched for. But when releasing music, *if you target your audience well,* you can use these ads to your advantage. We've learned about using demographic data and creating interest buckets through Meta to define target audiences. YouTube takes an exponential leap by making it possible to target *specific channels.*

With YouTube, you can advertise your recorder quartet release on a channel that specialises in recorder music or a related topic (teaching how to play the recorder, baroque music). You could even create a video advert that has content that is like the channel you are trying to target - like a score following video. A score following video is where someone uploads a video featuring the score of the music synced to the recording so you can read the music while listening to the recording. If someone is exploring a score following channel and your advert comes on, you have provided relevant and entertaining content for your customer – content that is like what they are expecting to see. Anything that from the customer's view adds value will capture the customer's attention much better than a direct sales pitch.

To use YouTube advertising, you need to create a video that you plan to use as an ad and upload it to your YouTube channel. It could be an unlisted video (not searchable, but the link can be shared by those who know it) or it could be public (for all to see), but it can't be private (viewable only by you or those whom you choose). Next, choose a *specific channel* on YouTube where you want to advertise, and link that video to your video ad.

Here is the link to the Google Advertising home page where you can sign up for an account and learn more about to how to use their service https://ads.google.com/home/. This is also on my resources page.

Google's ads can be as low as 1 penny a day, while ads on Facebook have a minimum cost of 1 pound a day. The more you spend, the larger the audience you can reach. The larger the audience the more data Meta or Google will collect about the people who engage with your content. And the more data that is collected, the more focused your targeting can be. This happens in the background. The more an advert is shown and engaged with, the more the platform 'understands' who that advert resonates with and therefore, who they should show it to. This is the learning phase of the advert.

In the first few days of posting an ad, the cost per click will be quite high as the learning phase of the advert happens and the platform gets a better understand of who engages with the advert. I've found good cost per click is about 10-20 pence, but this will change depending on whether you are charged for every click (a click-through campaign) or if you are charged only when someone performs the action you want them to take (conversion campaign). Conversion campaigns usually cost more than click-through campaigns, but if the cost per click doesn't exceed the cost of the product, then you will still be earning a profit. For example, if you are selling a CD at £10, but the cost per click is £6, that is still a £4 profit on the ad. This doesn't consider any of the other costs associated with the creation of a CD, but it gives you an idea that a 'good' cost per click is variable. It also doesn't consider the rule of seven. Your advert might trigger someone to remember to buy tickets for your next concert or tell a friend about your music.

Define and target your audience as specifically as possible and limit your investment or you will risk spending large amounts of money for little or no return. Online advertising is powerful, but like PR, it is a gamble.

Influencer marketing

This is an area of marketing that has grown over the last 10 years with the increased prevalence of social media. **Influencer marketing** is a marketing activity that employs someone to provide endorsements of your product to others within their social media sphere. Album reviews are a type of influencer marketing. In politics, an endorsement of your candidacy is another kind of influencer marketing. On a smaller scale, asking friends to promote your album and share it is also influencer marketing.

However, when people say, 'influencer marketing' in a professional sense, they are looking to engage someone with a large social media reach to promote their product in a way that seems organic based on the influencers' brand. Influencers spend a lot of time cultivating their following and then monetising it.

Like everything, if you take this route there will be a cost: usually a set fee per social media post. And you must work out if the benefit is worth the cost in doing it. Will it help you reach a new audience? Will your music suit the audience of that influencer? Is it a good brand match? For example, you might follow a streamer that plays *Dungeons and Dragons*. You have a track that has a kind of spooky tense feel to it that would be excellent for background music on one of the streamer's campaigns. You could contact that streamer and ask if they would be interested in using your music. If they choose it, then other people with similar interests will hear your music and maybe use it as background music for their own campaigns. This is an example of a synergy that is based on your own personal interest.

I don't have experience with this type of marketing, but it may be something you want to explore.

---

1. https://www.indeed.com/career-advice/career-development/rule-of-7-marketing

14

USING SOCIAL MEDIA TO PROMOTE YOUR MUSIC

Chapter 12 and 13 were about PR and marketing. This chapter is about how to build and leverage your already existing social media following to promote your music. There isn't a wrong way to do this, but however you do it you need to be comfortable with what you are sharing.

Engaging with your followers

Social media interactions need to be friendly, authentic, and informal. Post as often as you like, but don't just 'shout into the void'–engage with people. Social media doesn't work if it's a one-way street. It is *social* media, after all. Remember that you are guiding people along a journey and developing their interest in you and your music.

Many platforms measure the level of engagement to determine which posts to push. If you post content and then you engage with the responses, your posts will be ranked higher. For every post I make, I try and engage with at least three other posts that aren't mine through a 'like', reply, or re-tweet. The algorithms for every platform constantly change so there isn't a fixed rule that a 'like' is given more weight than a 'comment'.

Post informal updates about your recording or writing process, music you enjoy, concerts you've been to, the book you are reading, industry news, a meme, information that others in a similar position might find useful (knowing about this book for example), anything really. If you post about this book on social media, please tag me and I will likely share the comment and follow you. Organic advertising is still advertising so thank you in advance if you choose to give this book a shout out.

Share as much or as little about your personal life as you want. But be yourself. The more authentic you are, the more engaged your audience will be, and that will increase your reach. You can then leverage your reach to talk about your upcoming work. The persona you create on social media is part of your brand identity. Have a look through my social media and you'll probably get a very good idea of what I care about and am interested in. I try to share things about the music business that I find interesting (or rant worthy) and occasionally share information about my music or projects I've been working on. There are numerous composers whose timelines are filled with promotions for their upcoming concerts, or they engage only with people who have said something about their work or their concert. This approach is very insular and doesn't begin to leverage the power of social media.

During a release, timing is everything. Most platforms

now allow you to schedule posts in the future. However, you could consider using services like Hootsuit or Buffer that combine social media channels, enabling you to post to more than one at the same time *and* schedule posts into the future. They can analyse when your followers are most active and suggest the best times to post content.

By posting regularly on social media channels, you will be in peoples' minds. I've had work come through because someone saw a post of mine on Twitter (when it was still Twitter!) or Instagram, and they contacted me. They already knew about me and my skillset because of my posts, but it was the timing that clinched the job. It wasn't the first time they had seen my post. In fact, they had probably seen something at least seven times...

Setting up a pre-save campaign

A **pre-save campaign** is a marketing activity that allows potential customers to listen to a clip of your music before it's released and choose to save it to their library on release day, via a digital link, known as a **pre-save link**. Many streaming, including Apple Music, Amazon, Deezer, and Spotify enable pre-save links to work on their platforms.

Figure 14.1 Pre-save link landing page

Many of us have had the experience of walking into a store and saying, 'I know this product is coming out--can you put one aside for me please?'. The shop would then hold a copy of the product and notify you as soon as they received stock from the supplier.

It's the same concept with a pre-save link, only the store is online. You include the link in your promotional and marketing materials, mailing lists, social media, press releases, etc. People who are interested in your music will click on the link which will take them to a landing page with an embedded track preview (see Figure 14.1). The track preview is sourced from somewhere you define, generally Soundcloud or YouTube. If they like what they hear, they will click through to their music service provider where they are asked to sign into their streamer to activate the pre-save function. They will also be prompted to share their email address with the composer/musician (this is an excellent way to gather opt-in email addresses for your mailing list, which I'll talk about later). The album or single will then be added automatically to their libraries on release day.

Once someone 'likes' your music on Spotify (and other platforms), a green icon will appear next to the music. For services like Spotify which use many signifiers to 'feed the algorithm', having many 'likes' for an album could increase the chances of your music being playlisted by one of the editors. It also gives information on listening interests to the service which can be used for the algorithmically generated playlists. If Facebook has lookalike audiences, Spotify has sound-alike audiences. If Alice likes music X and Y, and Bob likes Y and Z, then Z will be recommended to Alice and X will be recommended to Bob because they both like Y, as depicted in Figure 14.2 on the next page.

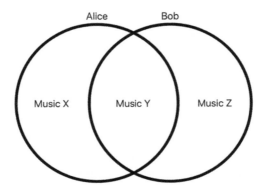

*Figure 14.2 Diagram showing how Spotify creates
'sound-alike' audiences.*

Some pre-save services allow you to embed a Facebook Pixel into your pre-save landing page.

This allows you to create adverts that:

1) re-target people who have clicked through to the pre-save link but have not yet added your album to their library,

2) remind people who have added it to their libraries to listen to your music or to buy a ticket for the release concert, and

3) create lookalike audiences based on people who have visited the pre-save link.

A pre-save link morphs into a smart link on release day. A smart link is like a pre-save link, but instead of asking people to 'save now', it changes to 'listen now', and takes the interested person directly to your music on that service. This is a valuable function because it allows you to use the same link pre- and post-release. You don't have to email journalists asking them to change the links they have in their articles or delete your social media posts that contain the pre-save link. You can also use this link in advertisements or social media posts you have scheduled in advance for release day knowing that the links in the posts will work and guide listeners to their preferred service.

Pre-save services can enable you to perform actions within a streaming platform. For example, Feature.fm allows users to 'follow an artist' or 'follow a playlist' through the pre-save link. Both actions are effective in building a following for future releases. Other platforms may follow suit–the streaming world is always evolving.

Using artificial intelligence

Artificial Intelligence (AI) is a rapidly developing field and is another tool you could use for promoting your work.

ChatGPT is an artificial intelligence chatbot (aka, a Large Language Model) developed by OpenAI. You can ask it questions in everyday language and you will get an answer. The free version has been trained on information up to year 2021, but newer paid-for versions have live access in real time to the internet. The better the question you ask ChatGPT, the better the answer. A new field related to ChatGPT is called 'prompt engineering'. It asks you to define the framework you want ChatGPT to work within and then you ask it a question within that framework.

Given you are reading a book about self-releasing your music, here are some examples of how you could use Chat GPT and the kind of prompts you could use:

'You are a social media executive. You are developing a

social media plan for an indie artist's first release. The album is called *Window*, contains five tracks, and is about window shopping. The target market for this album is 25–35-year-olds. This is the artist's bio [paste bio]. I want you to write a social media plan spanning one month to advertise the release, with suggested content for Facebook, Instagram, and X. In addition I want you to suggest ideas for video content specifically for TikTok. Ask me for any additional information you require'.

ChatGPT might then ask a few clarifying or probing questions before generating a series of content suggestions based on what you've told it. You can then take these suggestions, edit them for clarity and accuracy and use them to create a social media campaign.

I often use ChatGPT as a tool to get over the blank page syndrome. It is always easier to edit something that already exists. However, I would never recommend using ChatGPT content 'raw' without first reviewing and editing its outputs. There are huge copyright concerns around the use of Large Language Models using copyright data in their training set with intense lobbying of government happening from both sides. Also ChatGPT has a habit of making up information. So make sure to fact check everything it says. The technology is very exciting as a tool but is still evolving. Rapidly evolving.

Using playlists to attract new listeners

Playlists are an excellent way to reach new listeners. These can be your own playlists or user-generated playlists.

When making your own playlists, think of them as building context for your music. These playlists have two functions. The first is to 'teach the algorithm' the context for your music to increase the chances of your music appearing on algorithmically generated playlists or appearing as 'recommended' to someone creating a new playlist (think back to Alice and Bob earlier liking tracks X, Y and Z). The second function is to give you something to share besides your own music. Remember that effective promotional campaigns always give something of value to customers. Instead of shouting to everyone on social media to listen to your music, a subtler and more effective approach might be to say, 'listen to the music I like', or 'listen to the music that inspired my new album' or 'listen to the music I've been listening to while writing my book'. Add a track or two of yours within that playlist. Tag the other performers, composers or record labels featured within the playlist (be magnanimous and give), and they will likely share it with their followers as well, allowing you to reach their audience. If you shout about other people's work, they will shout about yours. Spread the love!

User-generated playlists are a little harder to break into. You can try and find the contact details of the person who owns the playlist. If they share their real name, a little bit of social media stalking can track them down and you can then send them one message and a follow up a few weeks later. Do not hassle people; it will turn them off if you are too pushy.

When I message people to include my music on their playlist, I often get a reply saying they'll include it for £50.

You might be tempted to take this offer–but don't! Paying for playlist placement is against all the streaming companies' terms of service and if they found out you have done so, your music will be removed. No matter how unlikely you think it might be that they would find out, don't risk it. It's not worth it.

You could also investigate SubmitHub or similar platforms that allow you to submit your music to curators and influencers, among other services. With SubmitHub, you buy credits and spend them to pitch your music to playlist curators who–to get paid a proportion of the value of the credit–listen to the track for a minimum amount of time. They also offer an option to give you feedback on the track you are submitting.

I've had some success with Submit Hub but have never been able to generate the same income as the cost of the pitch. Also, I don't know if any of the placements I got through SubmitHub have led to other more profitable placements. You might have more luck in a genre outside of classical music. I'm aware I work in a niche.

A free service called www.isitagoodplaylist.com asks you to paste a playlist link into the website and then shows you the market statistics for both the playlist and the individual tracks. This information helps you decide if a playlist is good or just looks good. A playlist could have loads of followers, but followers don't translate into streams. To work out how many followers of a playlist do translate into streams, you can look at the individual artist's Spotify pages and look at the 'Discovered On' section. If the playlist appears in multiple artists 'Discovered On' sections, and if these artists have many monthly listeners, then it increases the chances that it is a valuable playlist. Isitagooplaylist.com can do this work for you.

I have had excellent placements using all these methods and I've also wasted money on failed advertising and playlist pitch credits. Like everything linked to PR and marketing, it's an educated gamble.

Pitching pre-release

Spotify and Amazon allow you to pitch your music to their editors before release, known as a **pitching pre-release** (you'll first need to sign up for *Spotify for Artists* and *Amazon Music for Artists*, respectively).

Spotify and Amazon, along with Apple, YouTube, and Deezer, give you analytics tools that are useful in measuring your success, refining your strategy, and understanding your audience. These platforms measure basic information such as number of streams, geographic location, gender, and age range. Some of them get even more granular, tracking counties and cities. You could use this information for planning tours, advertising, and pitching.

Spotify for Artists will place your upcoming release prominently on the home page, once you log in, with a prompt to 'pitch to an editor'. In this section, you share information about the genre of your music along with mood, culture, and style references. The options to select from might seem confusing or irrelevant to your work. For example, the genre field invites you to enter your genre into the search bar. Naturally, I typed in 'classical', but this wasn't an option; it was the main heading of a sub-headed series of selectable options, but not an option itself.

The list looked something like this:

<u>Classical</u>
- contemporary
- chamber
- minimal
- experimental

'Classical' wasn't selectable but 'chamber' was. By selecting 'chamber' you are saying it is 'classical – chamber'. (Let's not even start with the fact that 'classical' is a specific era of music!)

This was the same for all other genres. 'Electronic' was a main heading and the subheading 'ambient' was a selectable option. You need to scroll down to find the right (or best) heading and option for categorising your music.

Once you've completed the 'pitch to an editor' page, you will be asked to fill in a 500-character text box to give more information on the release, like what your marketing plans are or any interesting background to capture an editor's attention.

Filling out these forms increases the chances of your music being included in a playlist appropriate to your music... but doesn't guarantee it. However, it does increase the likelihood that your track will be pushed to your followers' Release Radar playlist, and your fans will be able to hear your track on the day it is released. You will recall that I highlighted one of the actions available through Feature.fm called 'follow artist'. More followers mean more Release Radar playlists for your new music. This will increase streaming numbers on release day and further define your music contextually, increasing the chance of other playlist placements and organic sharing. It is a virtuous cycle.

Amazon Music have allowed artists to pitch in a similar way. Log into the *Amazon Music for Artists* app and go to the user profile icon at the bottom right. Click on the icon and you will be taken to a page with an option to pitch your music. You can choose up to three genres and include 1,000 characters to describe your target audience and your music. You can also select up to three artists with similar music or a similar audience and select the mood of your music and what activities it matches (chilling out, gym, running, etc). You'll also get an option to record up to a 15-second introduction to your music.

Amazon uses this information to target potential customers through push notifications (for followers), genre-based browsing, and curated playlists. Since using this feature on a recent release, I've had a reasonable number of streams for the track I pitched, so I consider it a worthwhile investment in your time.

The question you might be asking is, how can I use these analytics platforms to reach and understand my listeners?

Using analytics

Analytics data that Amazon and other platforms collect provide an infinite number of combinations for identifying trends and targeting groups quickly and efficiently. Once you define an audience or multiple audiences, you can push advertisements tailored to those specific groups.

When I say, 'define an audience', this isn't something you do in the platform that shows you the analytics data–you must do it yourself: for example, you saw a spike in women between 30-34 listening to your music in Rome. You could then use that data to create an advert on Facebook or Google targeting that specific group. It might be that your music was broadcast on a station popular in that demographic or an article was written about you that you don't know about. You should use the data to capitalise on such an event and lean into the rule of seven.

Let's say you posted something on Instagram that had more than your normal amount of engagement. Over the subsequent week you saw a significant increase in streams on Spotify and Apple Music. Because of the level of engagement, you decide to use that post as an advertisement targeting the demographic of people that you have noticed listening to your music in the last week. You can continually test and refine what works and what doesn't.

If you're pitching for playlist placement and pitching for programming, you can use this data as statistical evidence that your music would be popular in a playlist or concert programme in a specific country, region, town, etc.

You could also use this data to pitch for funding. In 2020, I needed funds to travel to Australia to perform my music. I was able to use this data to prove that a high proportion of my streams were from Australia. I argued that going to Australia in person would give me the opportunity to set up profile-raising activities that would build on my existing base of followers. Use the data creatively to build your career.

Instagram and Facebook also provide demographic data about the people who follow you and engage with your posts. Other paid-for services, like Chartmetric and Soundcharts, track your data across all the major platforms: X / Twitter, Facebook, Instagram, TikTok, Wikipedia, YouTube, Soundcloud and all the streamers. Doing this allows you to see any correlation between a popular post you put out, leading to a bump in streaming numbers. You could then choose to use that post for an advert you might also analyse the post to see what it was about it that was so engaging so you can try to replicate it. Or was it just a random occurrence?

A word of caution: You can spend way too much time on analytics (it's fun), so choose what data points are most useful to you and how you can use them for the best return on investment of your time and money.

Website and mailing list

Unlike the channels and platforms we've discussed up to now, your website and mailing list are the only two online spaces where you have control over your content and how it's managed. With Facebook, Google, YouTube, etc., you have no control over the visibility of your post or if the algorithm works in your favour or if someone even shares your music. You either must pay to get in front of people, or you are at the mercy of the algorithm pushing (or not) your content based on arbitrary rules. A change in policies or programming could obliterate your existing connection and engagement with people. Every few years you'll see an article on how engagement/reach/views on posts have decreased on [insert platform name]. The reason? They have changed their delivery algorithm to keep people on the platform. I mentioned earlier that Facebook currently favours video content. This subsequently led to more videos being posted on Facebook as creators tried to engage with the policy change. It is always the same… a game of cat and mouse between platform and creator where a platform changes the rules, and the creator must change what they do to get the same reach.

If you don't have a website or a mailing list, start them today, before you do anything else in this book! Seriously, put the book down now, claim your domain name and sign up to Mailchimp. Do it before you forget, and inertia takes over.

WEBSITE

Your website can be simple or complex, but it must serve as the go-to place for information about you on the internet.

The simplest website should have:

1. headshot/promo photo
2. short biography
3. music – never auto playing! (If I open a website and it auto plays, I close it never to return.)
4. links to your social media
5. signup form to your mailing list

These five elements form the core of your website.

Anything else you add to the site needs to add value to your brand or else it's a distraction.

My website www.matthewwhiteside.co.uk is built using the self-hosted Wordpress website, and the plugin suite, WooCommerce. You can find many other plugins for different functions, but these two are the pillars of the website.

Wordpress is free if you install it on your own server or for a monthly fee if you use their hosting service, though a server does cost money in upkeep. You also need to buy a domain name for the website. I bought my domain and server from Ionos. Originally, Wordpress was built as a blogging platform, but you can adapt it to whatever you need by installing themes. A theme refers to a templated design someone else has made for the website that you can use. There are loads of good free themes, but you will have to buy the ones with additional functionality. If you know how to program, you could build them yourself.

Plugins are code you install on your website to perform a specific function, such as allowing you to embed streaming links or a Meta Pixel, add watermarks to downloadable pdfs or any other number of things. You could build them yourself if you know how, but generally you can use free plugins for everything you need. I think I've only paid for two plugins on my website.

WooCommerce is a free plugin for Wordpress that allows you to run an online store. I have set up the plugin on my site so that almost every page you look at is a product that can be sold–it's a searchable catalogue for my compositions. When I add a new composition, it will appear on the relevant pages (e.g., string quartets or violin). Each product page has all the information anyone might need about the composition, including a score follower, an audio clip of the work or a link to stream or buy the full track. If I choose, I can then add purchase information to these pages to allow customers to order the score as a digital or physical product and pay for it then and there.

The score-following videos are hosted on YouTube and link back to the relevant page on my website. Embedding links from YouTube provides multiple functions:

First, Google shows YouTube videos for the relevant search term at the top of search results. If you were to search for 'viola and electronics' on Google, my piece, *Ulation*, is currently the top video result (see Figure 14.3).

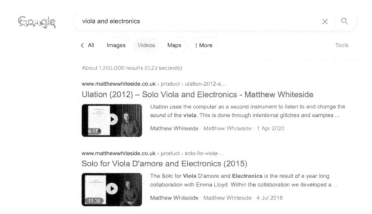

Figure 14.3 Google results for 'viola and electronics'. Accessed 1/12/2023

IT IS ALSO the top result for both search and video if you type in 'solo viola and electronics' (see Figure 14.4 below).

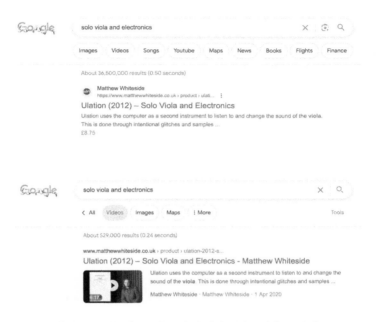

Figure 14.4 Google search results for 'solo viola and electronics'. Accessed 1/12/2023

Second, Google uses keywords, inbound and outbound links, length of content, style of writing and many more indicators to decide what to show users when they search. One of those indicators is how many references across the internet there are to that page. By linking from YouTube to your website you are building a reference to promote your website in the search results.

Third, hosting videos on YouTube allows for organic discovery on the platform or for using the videos as advertising assets, both of which feed back to your own website. Once people are on your website, you can target them with advertising to remind them that you exist ('Rule of Seven') or build audiences that have the same profile on other platforms.

Your website needs to be as discoverable as possible. If a reviewer, broadcaster, concert programmer, or potential customer can't find your website within the first two or three pages of Google results, you may as well not exist. As brutal as it sounds, it's true. If you want more information on how to increase your ranking in a search, Google 'Search Engine Optimisation' or 'SEO' or head to www.matthewwhiteside.co.uk/guidebook-resources where I've linked to a few more in depth guides.

If your website has popups that trigger instantly or music that starts playing automatically, you will drive people away. Always think from a user's point of view. I'm usually listening to music while working, so if your website starts playing music as soon as its loaded, I will close it immediately. The user needs to *choose* to listen. Use an embedded player hosted on YouTube or Soundcloud (if your music is unreleased) or Spotify / or Apple Music (if your music is already out).

Your website is much more than just a storage place for information. It can act as a data-gathering source (pixels) to build and understand your advertising audience. It can also be a storefront for your CDs, scores, concert tickets and merchandise.

MAILING LIST

Email is still one of the most popular communication platforms and one of the best ways to market to people. Your mailing list is the only guaranteed way to reach people who have an interest in your music. They have opted-in to hear about your news which is delivered directly to their inbox.

Because of strict data protection laws in the UK, opt-in is key. Make sure you get a clear indicator from people that you can add their email address to your mailing list. This could be verbal consent, an email consent form, or a mailing list sign-up sheet at a concert. I recommend creating a signup form on your website for your mailing list. The form could be presented as a popup or a footer that is triggered after a specified scroll time or time viewing the page.

Also make sure you have a clear opt-out on any emails you send as part of your list. At the bottom of every email that I send to my mailing list, I state: 'As a reminder, you are on this mailing list because at some point you expressed an interest in being kept up to date with my news. If you no longer want to be on this list, please unsubscribe below.' The 'unsubscribe' button is clearly shown a few lines lower. This will ensure you are compliant with data protection laws.

Never spam people or they will just unsubscribe or ignore your email. Again, think about the user's experience. For example, you might love your friends, but you don't want to hear what they are up to every single day. However, you do want to hear if something new or notable has happened in their lives. Use your mailing list in a similar way, to share selected news like a new album launch or a series of concerts. You could also send an email on the same day every month. These strategies will cut the risk that your email is treated like spam. The audience will look forward to receiving the monthly email.

Mailchimp is an excellent way to run your mailing list. It is free for up to 500 contacts, or a monthly fee for larger contact books. It can also sync with your website if you are running your website as an online shop. This syncing allows Mailchimp to act like a customer relationship manager (CRM) tool, monitoring your contacts to track buying behaviour on your website and prompting people to sign up to your mailing list at checkout. You could then segment your mailing list and give discount codes or early bird access to people who have bought your music. Think of how to make them feel special and valued. This will help you build a following of fans, not just one-off sales.

Having a mailing list is a major tool for reaching and developing your target market and building your business. Start one now.

15

SYNCHRONISATION

Synchronisation (or Sync) is the act of licensing music for placement in film or TV. This can be an excellent way to earn substantial amounts of money from your recorded music. However, success in synchronisation lies in your ability to build relationships with the right people at the right time or to build your reputation and cultural clout to the point where you get asked for the music.

Producers, directors, film editors or music supervisors have input into the music for the production. If you know any of these people and they like your music, you have a much better chance of being chosen. This is only true of recorded and already released music. If you have just written your work but don't have a fully mastered recording, there is no chance of your music being used. If you try and pitch it, it might even harm your chances for future work because you will come across as amateurish. The world of sync can move very fast. No music supervisor wants to take a chance on someone inexperienced in case there is a legal or rights issue that comes back to bite them.

Synchronisation deals cover all the rights within a piece of recorded music (the composition, the publisher, the performer, and the master). In the UK, most TV companies have a blanket license from PRS, MCPS and PPL so they can use almost any music ever released within their productions for UK broadcast. The allocation of royalties is a simple process, and you'll learn that your music was used in a synchronisation only after a royalty payment comes in.

However, in the US, each piece of music for synchronisation needs to be negotiated. If all the rights reside with one person or there is one person authorised to act on behalf of every rights holder, then the track is said to be a One Stop Shop. The production group can approach this one person for permission to use the piece and to negotiate the fee (clear the track).

If the rights are owned by different people, it can become much more complicated because everyone needs to agree that the track can be used in the production. If you have one rights holder who owns 1% of the composition copyright who is either unreachable or who refuses to allow the usage, the deal will fall through. The speed at which these deals can happen is scary. A film might be in the process of being edited to your track and the movie producer needs to know if they can clear it before they carry on with the edit. If they can't clear it in a reasonable amount of time (or sometimes unreasonable, like 30 minutes), they will move onto something they can clear.

This sounds like a lot of stress, but the pay-out can be

worth it. For the right track in the right placement the sync fee alone is in the thousands or hundreds of thousands of dollars. If you are a small, relatively unknown artist, then you will be on the lower end of the scale. If you are a world-famous pop star, then you will be on the upper end of the scale.

Duration, exclusivity, and where the film will be released will also change the fee. For example, a worldwide release with exclusivity for 10 years would capture a higher fee than a non-exclusive local release. Exclusivity in this sense means you cannot use that track for another synchronisation. Exclusivity could also refer to both the underlying composition and master or just a specific master (this is what Taylor Swift is doing, re-recording her works to own the master rights).

In sync, they talk about the 'two sides to every sync'. This refers to the composition and the master. If you are offered $5,000 per side, that means $5,000 to the composition side and $5,000 to the master. The composition is split between the composer and the publisher (if you don't have a publisher, you keep it all). The master goes to the record label. On top of this, the Musicians' Union will negotiate a separate fee for the secondary use of the musicians' performance which will be paid by the production company (you agreed to this in the MU/BPI session agreement), though the production company sometimes tries to negotiate for this to be paid from the total sync fee. If this happens, you should push back as hard as you can. In sync, almost everything is negotiable.

A secondary use is simply a subsequent use of music in addition to its primary usage. For example if a recording was made for an album release, then a secondary usage would be a sync or if a recording was made for a film a secondary usage could be the album release.

An additional cut might go to a sync agent if you have one. A sync agent works at networking with directors and music supervisors to understand what productions are in progress and pitching music that could be fitting for the production. They are often also on a sizable number of mailing lists to get direct briefs from the music supervision teams they have relationships with. A sync agent will take a percentage cut of any fee they bring in which could be between 20% and 50%. Sync agents might also work on a retainer model where you pay them a set fee every month or year and they take a lower percentage. Again, it depends on what deal you have negotiated with them.

If you are a composer (without a publisher) who performed on your own work and have released it yourself, and you were offered $5,000 a side you would get a $10,000 fee for the usage of your work. That fee doesn't include broadcast royalties or additional streams and sales (and potentially more syncs) because of the increased profile of your music. A sync is not the end of the story. A sync will increase your royalties and raise your profile. You can use the tricks outlined in earlier chapter to capitalise on this increased profile (rule of seven).

Be careful with any sync deal regarding exclusivity. Production companies may ask for exclusive use of the track for a certain period, in a certain country, on certain media or in a specific context. This is more likely when it comes to advertising than film and TV. If there is any exclusivity involved, then the fee to use the music will be higher compared to non-exclusive use. There is nothing wrong with exclusivity you just need to know what you are signing. It is all up for negotiation though. You should have a friendly lawyer on speed dial or use something like the Musicians' Union contract checking service which is free to members.

A sync can be an excellent upfront earner with back-end broadcast royalties as icing on the cake. I've had some success with getting my music placed and have also started to work as a sync agent, representing and pitching contemporary classical music to productions. It is a long, relationship based, game.

PART III

INDUSTRY THOUGHTS

Everything in the book up to this point has been focused on how to release your own music. You don't need to read on if that's all you want. However, the next section is a deeper dive into the history and ethics of streaming and my comments on the music business. I hope you find it interesting and informative.

16

THE ETHICS OF STREAMING

N o book about releasing your own music would be complete without a discussion of the industry ecosystem and the massive problems with it, including lack of fair payment, general exploitation, and missing credit where it is due. This is especially true for independent artists. Let's look at how we got to where we are today and what you can do about it.

Spotify
In the early 21st century, the music industry went through a massive paradigm shift. Technology and digital advancements led people to consume music differently. Instead of paying for and downloading individual music files or buying CDs, people started subscribing to online music curators and distributors. Streaming became the norm for listening to music. Spotify set itself up as the 'solution' for the record industry, and for better or worse, they did permanently transform the business. But their

deals have cast a long shadow over the music industry. Where did Spotify come from?

Spotify was originally designed as a platform to distribute content across users in a peer-to-peer network. The type of content was inconsequential. It was the platform and its functionality that mattered. As time went on, the founders started looking for other business opportunities for the platform.[1]

In their 2007 US patent application, Spotify requested that their platform be allowed to represent all digital content, including music and video.[2] Spotify had set its sights on becoming a video distribution company (the paradigm shifts also transformed the video industry). However, bandwidth requirements proved to be too big an obstacle, and Spotify shifted their focus to music sharing. This is how Spotify stumbled into the music business.

To start, they accessed music files that were on their employees' private computers. Many of these files were '...downloaded through file-sharing services... Rights holders had not granted the company the licenses required to distribute files online.'[3]

You could say that Spotify started off as a 'pirate service'[4], developing their company off the backs of other peoples' creativity. Not quite the rosy I-set-up-Spotify-to-save-the-music-industry spiel that the CEO, Daniel Ek, is often quoted as saying.

Unfortunately, this is a common theme throughout recorded music history. People's ability to exploit the art moves faster than the ability to monetise or legislate for the protection of creators and performers.

Spotify grew quickly in a private beta. In early 2008,

they had the aim to 'make music free by relying entirely on advertising'.[5] In October of 2008, Spotify started putting in place the licenses required to legally use the music they were already providing. That means that from 2006 to October 2008, Spotify had no licenses.

Spotify slowly expanded across the world, but it took them a while to license their service to pay out composition royalties. If the composer or songwriter wasn't signed to a major label with an income split specified from the sale of the tracks, then they wouldn't see any money at all. This changed only when Spotify was granted a license from PROs to allocate streaming royalties from around the world.

There was a huge amount of hype around Spotify, and the record labels didn't want to be left behind (even if their composers were). The major labels set up licensing deals with Spotify to ensure they were paid for their catalogues on the platform. These deals were (and new iterations of them still are) closely guarded commercial secrets, but we can get hints of them and their logic through the pro-rata system that we are currently working within.

Understanding the history of Spotify is key in understanding the current streaming business. Spotify Teardown by Maria Eriksson, Rasmus Fleischer, Anna Johansson, Pelle Snickars and Patrick Vanderau is a fascinating insight into the company. So fascinating, the book opens with a cease-and-desist order from Spotify sent to the researchers. They carried on and published in 2019. This gives you a flavour of the music industry and its secretive nature.

Pro-rata system

In a **pro-rata system**, the royalties from streaming are put into a common 'pot'. That pot is then divided by the number of streams that reach a given duration (usually 30 seconds) in a certain period. Therefore, a royalty paid on a track that is 31 seconds long would be the same as a track that is 31 minutes long because both are seen as one stream.

The system takes all the money brought in during a period (usually 28 days), minus a 30% platform fee, and divides that remaining 70% by the number of streams that hit a given duration (generally 30 seconds) and pays that out to the various rights holders. If the platform brought in £100,000 in a 28-day period and had 6,000,000 streams, it would keep £30,000; the remaining £70,000 would be divided by 6,000,000 thus giving a price per stream of about £0.012. That £0.012 is then paid out to the composers, publishers, and record labels (see table below). The actual splits are subject to non-disclosure agreements.

Total income	Distributable income (minus 30% platform fee)	Total streams	Price per stream
£100,000	£70,000	6,000,000	£0.012

Split of income in pro-rata system

This works well for a record company with a massive catalogue spanning millions of tracks; a catalogue that includes the most popular music ever released alongside new music they hope will grow to have the same impact; a catalogue where they pay the performers directly through a royalty split. It is a way for them to hedge their income and ensure they get a nice chunk of the income whatever way their tastes shift.

Hedging is a financial term where one risky investment is offset by another, linked, investment. A great example of this is the story of Mattress Mack, a furniture salesman in Texas. He makes offers on his products such as $1,000 dollars refunded if his favourite team, the Houston Astros, win. To hedge against this offer he bets on the Houston Astros winning. If they win, he can give the offer money out at no cost to him. If they lose, he still has the sales in his pocket. Either way, he gains from the marketing exposure through the offer and doesn't lose any money that isn't an investment in promoting his business. A marketing expense.

If you put yourself into the shoes of a record label executive negotiating a pro-rata license, you can understand why they would hedge their bets: to survive and profit. But it is this very license we are now having to unpick and lobby to change.

I'd like to share with you the top line figures I have from 6 months of streaming data from January to June 2019 (see table below).

Payment Source	Streams	Total Payment	Average per stream
Distributor/Aggregator	7894	£35.03	£0.004438
PRS	3322	£1.5508	£0.00046683
MCPS	1550	£1.085	£0.0007
		Total	£0.0056

Average value of my streams through the pro-rata system

This is an amalgamated amount from every source from around the world that streams my music. I am not sharing this to compare one company to another but rather to demonstrate the overall problem with the system.

I can see these numbers in their entirety because I am a composer who self-releases his own music. Even so, these took a few days to sift through to find out the average value of a stream.

In April 2019, I had a total of 68 streams from Canada on Apple Music. 50 of these were paid out at an average of £0.005152 while 18 were paid out at an average of £0.002771. In the same period, 12 streams in Japan averaged £0.003929 while 12 streams in Switzerland averaged £0.008251.

You can see the massive disparity in total streams in the same period from different payment methods. As an independent composer and record label, it is impossible to link a royalty payment from PRS or MCPS to a specific streaming payment from my distributor because the system doesn't share the data that allows you to track a specific player's royalties.

While my distributor will send an earnings report

showing line-by-line royalty payments, the international PROs won't. Their individual distribution policies dictate how royalties will be paid. Some PROs only distribute when a rights holder earns above a minimum threshold in each payment period. If the rights holder's earnings don't hit the threshold, then the money gets put into a black box and divided by market share (in other words those with the most streams will suck up the most undistributed money). Other PROs will distribute everything earned within that same period. There's no transparency in the calculations. I have tried.

In November 2023, Spotify announced that from early 2024 they would only start to pay out once a track has had 1,000 streams in a year.[6] I feel the language around this announcement is quite insulting for those working in niche genre or just starting out and, what's more, they only consulted the major record labels before going ahead with this change. None of the professional organisations representing freelancers or independent record labels were consulted. There are also questions around the legality of this in the UK. In my view, by de-monetising tracks under a certain play count, they are effectively stealing the masters. I have spoken to PRS and MCPS and, thankfully, there is nothing changing with regards to the composition licensing. We will wait to see how this plays out.

This is the stark reality of self-releasing. You are at the behest of policies over which you have little or no influence, and it is impossible to find out how much money you haven't been paid because of the calculations and distribution policies that are subject to non-disclosure clauses.

UNFAIR TO THE USER

The pro-rata system is grossly unfair, not only to the music-makers, but also to the music-listeners. It incentivises shorter works and penalises long-form music, and doesn't give consumers full value for their money. For example, users mainly pay a £9.99 subscription fee every month. Spotify keeps about £3 of that to cover their costs. Fine, they need to pay their staff and keep the servers running. But the user that listened to one track in a month still only triggers one payment and that payment is a proportion of the larger bucket. Based on my earlier calculations, a stream is worth c. £0.0056, so where does the other £6.9944 go? To popular music! The licenses that the major labels negotiated are essentially massive pyramid schemes where the money flows up to the top.

This isn't just a Spotify problem; this applies to most streaming companies. Spotify developed the standard payment models that every other company then followed. And given the way Spotify developed as a business, should they have been the ones to create the awful precedent that is near impossible to shift? But how bad is it, really? What are the larger implications for music under a pro-rata system? We need to start thinking about reasonable listening amounts and how they amalgamate to a make a total distribution amount, rather than just one stream per month in isolation to start to answer this.

Before we do that I need to acknowledge that Spotify

increased their subscription to £10.99 in July 2023 and Apple Music in October 2022. However, I haven't seen the knock-on effect of this increase in royalties yet. So, I have left reference to subscription amounts as £9.99 for the rest of this chapter because the figures I have access to are from a period when £9.99 was the norm for both Spotify and Apple Music.

Say you are someone who only listened to music on your commute to and from work and for a few hours at the weekend. We will assume two hours a day during the week and four hours at the weekend totalling 18 hours listening time a week.

According to the Statista website, the average track length in 2020 was three minutes and 17 seconds.[7] This means in your 18 hours (1080 minutes) of listening to music, you would trigger 328.9 payments. This would be a weekly total payment triggered of about £1.84 or about £7.36 a month. That's based on my own averages I shared at the start of this chapter. This is within the ballpark of what someone could reasonably listen to in a month and is paying out broadly what they are paying into the system with their subscription. This sounds totally fine, fair, and reasonable.

Where it starts to become problematic is if your musical tastes differ at all from this average...

I'VE SCROLLED to a random point on my iTunes music library to the songs I've listened to more than five times and these five tracks are together:

- 'Go A' by Shum: 2min 53
- 'Asyla. III'by Thomas Adés: 6min 21
- 'Unbreakable Silence' by Ben Frost & Daniel Bjarnasson: 3min 37
- 'Face to Face/Short Circuit' by Daft Punk: 4min 56
- 'Ljiraq' by Dawn of Midi: 5min 2

The total play time of the music stream is 23 minutes 9 seconds, and the average track length is 4 minutes 38 seconds. In the 18 hours of listening, I'd trigger 233 payments a week, 932 a month or total payments of about £5.22 a month. Lower than the c. £7 cut off for payments—not a discrepancy most users would complain about, but multiplied by millions of users, it becomes a huge source of income for someone. Who? Well, hold that thought for a moment. There is one more, even worse example to show you.

The real problem is for any long form music (like most classical music, or even more experimental popular music like Pink Floyd's Echoes at 16 minutes). Using the same 18h a week listening time for 10-minute tracks, you'd trigger 108 payments a week, 432 a month or £2.42 a month.

The difference between your subscription fee of about £10 a month and what you trigger (£2.42) doesn't just go to the streaming company. Thanks to the pro-rata system, it is allocated to music you haven't even listened to. It is thrown into the massive pot! This means that if you only listen to 10-minute tracks in a month, most of your money is going to popular artists–trickle up economics that completely misrepresent the relationship between listener and musician!

There is a better way. It's called the user-centric payment system.

User-centric

The **user-centric payment system** is the way that most listeners assume their royalties are paid to rights holders. In a user-centric system, a user's subscription money, minus a platform fee, gets paid to the people involved in the creation of the music that is streamed. If a listener streams one track in a month, they pay c.£7 to the rights holders involved; if they stream 200 tracks, they trigger 200 payments of £0.035. This represents the correct relationship between the listener and the rights holders and greatly reduces the chance of streaming fraud. Try and describe the pro-rata system to someone streaming music, and they will be shocked and that's only if they can get their head around it! The user-centric system is not only simple and straightforward, but also sensible and fair. It is the way it should have been from the start.

The biggest criticism of user-centric methods is that a value of a user's stream is variable, but this already happens on a month-by-month basis (as I've shown in my example from Canada earlier) and to me, this change is fair. The value of a stream should change, the value of a user's subscription shouldn't. A 30-minute track shouldn't be 'worth' the same amount as a 3-minute one. This is no value judgement on artistic quality but simply on how much attention (measured in minutes) it takes for someone to listen to the music.

If someone told you that you would be paid the same amount every month no matter how many hours you work, you would either work out how to game the system or leave for a company that pays more fairly.

The bigger streaming companies that use the pro-rata model argue that it would be impossible to change to user-centric; the change wouldn't have the desired result of fairer payments to rightsholders, and it would cost too much. Soundcloud have completely debunked this through their fan-powered royalty model (a.k.a., user-centric) and the research they have published shows how it would benefit niche, long-form, and early career musicians because '64% of artists with between 100 and 1,000 listeners earned more from FPR than they would have from pro-rata'.[8]

User-centric allows for more varied types of music to be financially viable. With the cost of digital shelf space being almost zero, every type of music can find its audience in the billions of listeners around the world and, importantly, flourish. The pro-rata system completely stifles this.

User-centric is also much easier to police because a user can never pay out more than they put into the system. In 2018 there were reports of 'The Bulgarian Scam'[9], so called because the ISRCs were registered in Bulgaria. A playlister had created a series of playlists that at first looked like a 'normal' playlist. But as you scrolled further down, the tracks got shorter and shorter and eventually were just white noise or silence of 31 secs long.

This playlister then pointed a bot farm of 1,200 pro Spotify accounts to stream these playlists constantly. These cost £12,000 a month but if they were only streaming tracks 31 seconds long, they would each trigger 2,787 streams a month totalling 33,444,000 streams. Based on a stream being worth £0.0056 they were triggering payments of a massive £187,286! The only reason this was discovered was because the playlist was so popular internally in Spotify, they looked at it. If they had done this over more playlists there is a chance no one would have noticed. Music Business Worldwide go into a lot more depth on this scam that wouldn't be at all possible under a user-centric system. Check out their article here: https://www.musicbusinessworldwide.com/great-big-spotify-scam-bulgarian-playlister-swindle-way-fortune-streaming-service/

Equitable remuneration

Equitable remuneration is another payment model that is based on the PPL royalties that performers get from radio and TV broadcasts.

Historically, a musician would be signed to a label and would be paid a cut of all sales. This was great for the featured artists, but not so much for the session musicians. Instead, the session musicians might only have been paid a session fee. The 1988 Copyright, Designs and Patents Act was signed in the UK which brought in Equitable Remuneration for performers. Then from 1996, PPL distributed royalties directly to musicians, though they had been distributing to record labels since the 1930s, for the use of their recordings on radio and then TV. Nowadays, even featured artists can't make a decent income from streams.

Equitable remuneration for streaming does not yet exist in the UK or the US. When it does, it will be another royalty payment paid by the relevant platform and collected by PPL or its sister agencies across the world. This payment would be paid directly to the musicians, ensuring that any legacy contracts that mention physical sales only would have to encompass digital sales so that session musicians would get their share of streaming income.

In late 2021, Kevin Brennan introduced a Private Members Bill to the UK Parliament requesting that equitable remuneration be expanded to include streaming. Unfortunately, the first reading didn't get passed; however, the Government did agree to an inquiry into streaming by the competitions commission. Preliminary results were released in late 2022. Unfortunately, the scope of the inquiry was to investigate the streaming market from the point of view of consumers. Unsurprisingly, they found that the streaming market was excellent for consumers because it provided unlimited choice for a reasonable subscription fee.

But they ignored the other part of the transaction: artists and record labels! A free market requires choice. Consumers can choose from among Spotify, Apple Music, Deezer, YouTube Music, Tidal, etc., but an artist must release on *all* of them (to make sure they reach their listeners), with no transparency into how the royalties in the collective 'pot' are distributed. There used to be exclusive deals for new releases on a specific platform for renowned artists, but this has stopped. Artists don't have the freedom to choose how or how much they are paid.

Here's an analogy: A manufacturer of car parts will choose a shipping company that charges the lowest price while providing the highest quality of service delivering goods on time and undamaged. Multiple shipping companies could deliver the goods to the same shops. But the car part manufacturer can choose the shipping company that they believe is the best one for their business. The customer then goes to the store where they want to make their purchase based on price, convenience, incentives, and other factors.

However, independent artists don't have a choice. They want their music stocked in every shop front, but every shop front will only select deliveries from one company. If the artist wants their music available to as wide an audience as possible, they will have to use every possible delivery company and just accept whatever terms are offered. It would be as if the car part manufacturer had to use Royal Mail as well as every other delivery company to get their products to the shop. In this analogy, the streaming company is the shop with an exclusive agreement from a delivery company and independent artists are the consumers who are paying (through a percentage cut) to get their product delivered. The artists have very little choice how the 'shop' pays them for their music because they will have to accept the terms. This is why I think both artists/labels and consumers of music should be classed as customers of the streaming company and why the remit of the inquiry fell short of its task.

Subscription fees

Most streaming services charge ~£10 for monthly subscription fee and have charged this same fee from the moment they were set up. Inflation devalues this fixed fee as the years go by. Using the Bank of England's Inflation calculator, £10 in 2006 would be £16.12 in March 2023– so about 60% higher than it is. If this translated through to royalty payments, an average payment would be about £0.01 rather than £0.0056! Multiple issues have converged to affect music as a viable business. I believe all of them can be fixed very easily. There just needs to be the commercial and/or political will to make the changes.

On the positive side, both Apple and Spotify have recently increased their subscription fees to £10.99. Less than inflation but still a positive move. Will that increase in subscription payments translate to a proportionate increase in royalties to rights holders, or just increase the money going to the head of the tail? We will wait to see.

I started these industry section saying that Spotify was both the problem and the solution in the music business. Their impact on the economics of streaming has cast a dark shadow over the industry. Musicians, composers, and songwriters deserve a payment method that is fair. However, if Spotify didn't appear and create a streaming market when they did, the recorded music industry could well have imploded. Food for thought.

What you can do

You might be feeling disheartened by this section at the end of a book where I've been guiding you on how to release your own music. The streaming earnings are not nice or encouraging, but once I understood the weird pyramid system I was working in, I was even more motivated to write this book and to campaign. I want you to be aware–not just about how to release your music, but also about the system you will be working within and how it is stacked against independent artists. Even signing to a label isn't going to help, because a label isn't going to be interested in you until you have some level of success. They want to reduce the risk of their investment. They are focused on making a profit.

However, there is a change in the air with Universal Music Group looking at shifting to implement an artist centric (aka, user-centric) payment system[10]. You can be part of this change through lobbying and educating your audience. Take part in #brokenrecord (led by Tom Gray) and #fixstreaming (led by the Musicians' Union). Teach your audience about why the Artist Centric/User Centric model is fairer and a more transparent system for distributing royalties. Write to your MPs about why legislating for a model that combines Equitable Renumeration and User-centric principles will help the music industry to thrive in the UK.

Changing payment models requires increased awareness in customers about the inequities in the system. Currently, the big companies are winning the PR battle in the market because they have the resources to keep the status quo. But if we as musicians, artists, and independent record labels shout with one voice, with one demand, then things *will* change. Either the streaming companies will change their practices based on market pressure or lost business, or we can force legislative change. Either way the answer to what you can do is simple. Lobby and educate!

1. Eriksson, Maria, et al. *Spotify Teardown: Inside the Black Box of Streaming Music.* Cambridge, Ma, MIT Press, 2019. P41
2. Andreas Ehn et al., "Peer-to-Peer Streaming of Media Content," US Patent 8,316,146, filed July 13, 2007, and issued November 20, 2012,
3. *Spotify Teardown.* P43
4. *Spotify Teardown.* P43
5. Spotify Teardown. P44
6. https://artists.spotify.com/blog/modernizing-our-royalty-system
7. https://www.statista.com/chart/26546/mean-song-duration-of-currently-streamable-songs-by-year-of-release/
8. https://musically.com/2022/07/13/how-do-soundclouds-fan-powered-royalties-work-for-artists/
9. https://www.musicbusinessworldwide.com/great-big-spotify-scam-bulgarian-playlister-swindle-way-fortune-streaming-service/
10. https://www.musicbusinessworldwide.com/sir-lucian-grainge-on-rewarding-real-artists-universals-global-expansion-strategy-and-more-from-the-companys-q2-earnings-call1

17

THE LONG TAIL

Chris Anderson's 2006 book, *The Long Tail*, illustrates how, thanks to digitisation and the internet, businesses can profit by offering a plethora of searchable products to the consumer. Businesses no longer need blockbuster products to profit. Selling a million different products a year can yield a huge return on investment in an age where physical inventory and storefronts, and the linked costs, have been replaced by digital products or avatars of physical products sold online at a fraction of the cost of keeping the physical product in a shop.

In this digital age, billions of products are discoverable and deliverable in a matter of seconds. Music that never had the chance of being listened to can be searched, purchased, and streamed. However, as I explained earlier, royalty payments in the pro-rata system are disproportionately taken from the niche label earnings (the long tail) to fund the ongoing production and promotion of big label blockbusters (the head of the tail).

Amazon transformed the book industry just as Spotify transformed the music industry. However, in contrast with the music business, author royalties aren't pooled and distributed inequitably, but are paid out per the terms of the publisher agreements. And the transactions are transparent.

I highly recommend *The Long Tail*. It dives into the economics of our world and the fragmented psychosocial aspects of our society. To me, this fragmentation is a good thing, as it means we are now able to acknowledge a wide spectrum of interests as well as cater to them. Niche groups want to connect with the niche products that interest them. These products have a place in our economy in the long tail, thanks to the internet. With the cost of digital shelf space and searching those shelves being almost zero, these niches should thrive. Like-minded people can now connect with like-minded people and build communities and viable businesses through the internet. It isn't just economics, it is everything. But isn't that economics?

18

RECORD COMPANIES AS INVESTORS AND ROYALTY-EARNERS

I n the initial deals with the record companies, Spotify often offered a share purchase option in addition to an upfront payment. Not only were (and in most cases still are) the major record companies being paid on streams; they also had an interest in Spotify growing the business so they could divest at a profit when Spotify was listed (Sony sold about half of its shares in Spotify during the first month of trading).[1]

Like most corporations, Spotify works at keeping costs low to be profitable and to pay dividends to investors and/or to reinvest earnings in the company to increase its market value. Spotify's biggest cost is royalties, but they also need to provide a good return to their investors. This creates a major conflict of interest when the investors are the biggest receivers of royalty payments for streaming content. Where do you think Spotify will cut costs to make investors happy?

Cherie Hu is an award-winning journalist who studies the connection between technology and music. She has done extensive research into record companies that invest in streaming companies and streaming companies that invest in each other. She has uncovered a complicated network of incestuous business deals, with companies owning a percentage of themselves through a third party (e.g., Spotify owns some of Tencent, Tencent owns a share of Sony, Sony owns a share of Spotify). These relationships make it extremely difficult to track down the movement of money, the payment of royalties, or provide musicians with any sort of transparency in the process.[2]

Companies have always used music to achieve other ends: to gain political capital and soft power, to sell products, to increase intelligence, to sell hardware, and ultimately, to make a profit.

For example, Apple is worth over $2 trillion. The profitability of their music sales is inconsequential to their overall business. Apple can easily afford to take a loss on music sales to sell their hardware, which brings in enormous profit. Music can be a loss leader to Apple.

A loss leader is a desirable product that can be used to draw a consumer in to purchase a higher priced or more profitable one. This happens a lot through offers being advertised that bring people into a shop and then, while in the shop, upselling or hoping they will buy something else that is more profitable while they are there.

A recent trend in the investment markets is for investment companies to purchase music rights. The biggest company is Hipgnosis Songs Fund, currently worth nearly £1 billion. Over the past few years, Hipgnosis focused on buying up the rights for compositions and recordings. Their aim is to generate an income from the catalogues and in turn create '...music as an asset class, just like oil or gold'.[3] They seem to be concentrating on the music of older musicians who want to cash out and enjoy their retirement but whose compositions will still be generating income for many years to come. On the one hand, this is a way for a musician to retire and not have to keep touring. On the other hand, Hipgnosis is becoming a publishing company through the back door. They are using their market position to lobby for fairer royalty payments for rights' holders, arguing that higher royalty payments will benefit everyone who is releasing music. This is obviously true and has a large amount of self-interest for their shareholders. But what could happen if they become a dominant player and start making demands that compromise the livelihoods of musicians? Will they become just another major publishing company? I haven't been able to work out the end goal for Hipgnosis, but for now, if you want to own a small proportion of Neil Young's music you can buy shares in Hipgnosis.

For transparency, I did own shares in Hipgnosis, but haven't since early 2022. Obviously, no part of this should be taken as investment advice.

---

1. https://variety.com/2018/biz/news/sony-has-sold-half-of-its-spotify-shares-1202794230/

2. https://www.hypebot.com/hypebot/2020/01/no-collusion-this-chart-show-the-music-industrys-incestuous-ownership-web.html

3. https://www.marketplace.org/2022/06/14/merck-mercuriadis-says-hit-songs-are-in-an-asset-class-all-their-own/

FINAL THOUGHTS

Congratulations. You know how to run a recording session, work out a budget, create a promotional strategy, develop your brand, and ultimately, to release your music into the world. You are better prepared to thrive in the music industry and negotiate a fair deal for yourself and you now understand some of the larger context of the business you are working within. Make sure to look at the additional resources on my website if you haven't already at www.matthewwhiteside.co.uk/guidebook-resources.

I know there are a lot of things to consider in pulling together a successful release strategy. But you don't have to do *everything* for your first release. Obviously, you need to do the technical side of things such as the registration and distribution, but you don't have to dive into the advertising as deeply as I've outlined. Even if you only do half of what is in this book, you'll still be doing a lot. You now know what is possible, and you can put this knowledge into action.

Get out there and fill the world with your music!

GLOSSARY OF KEY TERMS

Advertising: a marketing activity that communicates product information to the customer in a compelling way.

Cardioid microphone: a microphone that picks up sound from the front 180 degrees of the grill.

Copyright: a type of intellectual property right that gives the owner the exclusive right to sell, distribute, adapt, and perform a creative work.

Customer journey: the stages a customer goes through leading up to making a purchase and staying loyal to a brand.

Earned income is any income you earn from sales and streams, radio play, live concerts, and synchronisation licences.

Editing: the first stage of postproduction which involves piecing together one seamless performance from all the takes from the recording session.

Equitable remuneration: a royalty payment model based on the PPL royalties that performers get from radio and TV broadcasts.

Executive producer: the person who manages all the creative and technical aspects of a recording project and fundraises for it to happen.

Figure of Eight: microphones that pick-up sound equally in front and behind. The pattern it creates looks like a figure of 8.

Fixer: someone who books musicians for a recording session.

(GVL) label code: GVL (Gesellschaft für Verwertung von Leistungsschutzrechte) is the German version of PPL. Master rights owners need to get their GVL code to track and collect royalties in Germany.

Hypercardioid microphone: a microphone that picks up sound from the front and back of the grill.

Interest buckets: users of Facebook and Instagram who, based on data gathered from Meta's platforms, are categorised according to their shared interests.

Influencer marketing: a type of marketing activity that employs someone to provide endorsements of your product to others within their social media sphere.

International Standard Recording Code (ISRC): An ISRC is an eleven-character alphanumeric code that identifies a specific recording and is unique to that recording.

Live recording: a recording that captures a live performance in front of an audience.

Live Recording venue: any place you want to record that is not in a purpose-built recording studio and is not in front of a live audience.

Marketing: a process that focuses on gathering data from a specific demographic to define, target and develop customers and products.

Marketing campaign: the specific activities taken over a given period to engage the target audience.

Marketing funnel: a concept used in marketing campaigns to map out the customer journey and articulate what you want the customer to do at each stage, leading to the sale. This is visually depicted as a funnel, representing all the potential customers at the widest part of the funnel, narrowing down to those who purchase the product.

Mastering: the final stage in postproduction (following mixing) that sets the right dynamic range in the edited and mixed recording and prepares it for final distribution on the specific platform or format for your release.

Mastering engineer: the person responsible for mastering the final recording for release.

Master rights owner: the person or company who owns the rights to exploit the master of a recorded composition. Often this will be the record label.

Mechanical Copyright Protection Society (MCPS): The MCPS licenses and collects royalties on behalf of composers and rights holders for when works are mechanically reproduced; that is, reproducing a copyrighted work by mechanical means rather than creating the work in the first instance.

Mixing: the second stage of postproduction (following editing) that shapes the sounds of the edited recording, making sure the performance sounds as good as it can within the context of the project.

Mixing engineer: the person responsible for mixing the recorded work.

Monitoring: the musicians' ability to hear their own playing in real time as the sound is being recorded.

Music publishers: music publishers license and market compositions for all media, including film, television, and advertising. They also manage rentals and distribution, monitor work usage, and distribute some royalties.

Omni-directional microphone: a microphone that picks up sound in a 360-degree radius around the grill.

Performing Rights Society (PRS): The PRS protects copyright and collects royalties for composers and rights holders for live performances on TV, radio, and online streaming.

Phonographic Performance Limited (PPL): PPL is an organization that collects and distributes royalties on behalf of the record label and performers whenever the audio recording of the work is used on TV, radio or, in some parts of the world, streaming.

Pitching pre-release: a service offered by *Spotify for Artists* or *Amazon Music for Artists*, that allows members to pitch their music to the platforms' editors before release.

Postproduction: the stage in the self-releasing process that pertains to the processing of the raw, recorded music and preparing it for final release. Postproduction includes editing, mixing, and mastering.

Pre-save campaign: a marketing activity that allows potential customers to listen to your music before it's released, via a digital link.

Pre-save link: the digital link activated in a pre-save campaign.

Pro-rata system: a royalty payment system in which all royalties from streaming are put into a common 'pot'. That pot is then divided by the number of streams that reach a given duration in a certain period.

Public relations (PR): companies or individuals that focus on developing and sustaining a positive image of a brand or person through free channels, such as reviews, blogs, and articles.

Record producer: the person who works with the executive producer to plan the recording logistics and hiring decisions for musicians and other crew. The record producer makes the artistic decisions and gives performance direction during the recording session from the recording booth.

Recording engineer: the person responsible for operating the audio equipment in a recording session to achieve the desired sound as stipulated by the producer.

Recording studio: a commercial space specifically designed for capturing, mixing, and mastering sound.

Record label: an individual or company that funds the recording of music and promotes and sells it in various formats to make a profit.

Release date: the date when your music will be available for sale through the distributor.

Release strategy: the master plan that follows a timeline for the successful release of your music.

Royalties: and income stream for copyright holders.

Story: the narrative that public relations providers create to frame you and your work to engage both the media and potential customers.

Synchronisation: synchronisation (or Sync) is the act of licensing music for placement in film or TV.

Talkback: the way the producer in the control room communicates with those in the live room during the recording session (either through a speaker in the live room or via musicians' headphones).

Universal Product Code (UPC): the barcode used to track sales across platforms and shops and used by the Official Charts Company to create the chart list.

User-centric system: a royalty payment system in which a user's subscription money, minus a platform fee, gets paid to the people involved in the creation of the music they listen to.

ACKNOWLEDGMENTS

This book is the culmination of many years of experience working as a composer and recording and releasing music. Experience which would not have been possible without the support and shared knowledge countless musicians, teachers, friends, industry professionals, funders and support organisations. It is impossible to thank everyone individually but know that I am eternally grateful for your support over the years.

There are some people I do want to thank specifically. My editor, Laura Pearson. Laura has been an amazing and supportive sounding board throughout the process of writing this book. She has dealt with my weird turns of phrase and helped turn my thoughts into a coherent book to share my experience to support others.

A huge thank you to my Crowdfunders!

- Ailís Ní Ríain
- Andrew Conway
- Anselm McDonnell
- Anthony Fiumara
- Ben Payton
- Bernard Hughes
- Bernard Hughes
- Bill Sweeney

- Cameron Biles-Liddell
- Cameron Lam
- Chris Hutchings
- Christopher Mortlock
- Claire McCue
- D. L. Chappell
- Danny Saleeb
- Dave Falconer
- Emma Lloyd and John Hails
- Erin Thomson
- Garrett Shatzer
- Greg Harradine
- Harriet Wybor
- Hilary Brooks
- Jo May
- Julian Wagstaff
- Katherine Wren
- Keir Long
- Laurie Stras
- Nichola Scrutton
- Nick DeSylva
- Olivia Brown
- Paul Thompson
- Pete Furniss
- Pippa Reid-Foster
- Rebecca Rowe
- Salem Yateem
- Sarah Dacey
- Shirley Barr
- Shona Dryburgh
- Simon Hellewell

- Stephen Goss
- Susanne Olbrich
- Tim Cooper

Thanks to this group of people, the 40 other anonymous supporters, and Creative Scotland's Crowdmatch scheme: you all helped in the creation of this book.

Thank you to my reviewers - Iona Fyfe, Stuart MacRae, Robin Rimbaud and Matt Buttler who read through a draft of this book and gave some really useful pointers and advice from their own experiences.

And THANK YOU to you for reading this book. I hope it is useful in your journey to musical success.

ABOUT THE AUTHOR

Matthew Whiteside is a composer and Artistic Director of *The Night With...* concerts based in Glasgow. He was one of *The List's* Hot 100 for 2019 and in 2020 was named 'One to Watch Classical' by *The Scotsman*. He won the Scottish Music Industry Award for Creative Programming at the  Scottish Awards for New Music for the 2019 season of *The Night With...*, and in 2021 won the Award for the Recording of New Music sponsored by *VoxCarynx* for his work on *The Night With... Live Vol. One*.

His 2019 album *Entangled*, featuring three string quartets with electronic interludes, was described as "effective and unsettling" by *BBC Music Magazine* and as "post-minimal bold sparseness" by *The Herald*. Arcana.fm said, "It is refreshing to encounter a composer making albums with new classical music in this way, for when used imaginatively the format still has much to give".

Other works include *Night Thoughts*, commissioned by *Crash Ensemble* for New Music Dublin and shortlisted in the 2021 Scottish Awards for New Music; the short opera, *Little Black Lies*, commissioned by *Scottish Opera Connect*, with libretto by Helene Grøn; *Quartet No. 4 (Entangled)*, commissioned by the Institute of Physics for the Northern Ireland Science Festival; *This Too Shall Pass*, for *Juice Vocal Ensemble*; and *Ground, Air, Life*, commissioned by *the Glasgow Barons*.

Matthew also regularly lectures on music, composition, sound design, and the music industry as a whole. His focus is on promoting a DIY mentality within the art.

Along with his concert compositions, he composed the music for *Michael Palin's Quest for Artemisia*, broadcast on BBC 4, and has scored two feature films (*Anna Unbound* and *The Loudest Sound*) along with numerous shorts. His music was also used in Citizens Theatre production, *The Macbeths*.

Matthew is also an avid Scuba diver who frequently shares his underwater experiences on social media.

www.matthewwhiteside.co.uk /www.thenightwith.com

 facebook.com/mwhitesidecomp
 x.com/mwhiteside
instagram.com/mwhitesidecomp

Milton Keynes UK
Ingram Content Group UK Ltd.
UKHW010114071223
433879UK00004B/148